Men-at-Arms • 484

The Portuguese in the Age of Discoveries *c*.1340–1665

David Nicolle • Illustrated by Gerry & Sam Embleton

Series editor Martin Windrow

First published in Great Britain in 2012 by Osprey Publishing,
Midland House, West Way, Botley, Oxford, OX2 0PH, UK
44-02 23rd Street, Suite 219, Long Island City, NY 11101, USA
E-mail: info@ospreypublishing.com
OSPREY PUBLISHING IS PART OF THE OSPREY GROUP

A CIP catalogue record for this book is available from the British Library

Print ISBN: 978 1 84908 848 0
PDF ebook ISBN: 978 1 84908 849 7
ePub ebook ISBN: 978 1 78200 323 6

Editor: Martin Windrow
Index by Sandra Shotter
Typeset in Helvetica Neue and ITC New Baskerville
Maps by the author
Originated by PDQ Media, Bungay, UK

Printed in China through Worldprint Ltd

12 13 14 15 16 10 9 8 7 6 5 4 3 2 1

Osprey Publishing is supporting the Woodland Trust, the UK's leading
woodland conservation charity, by funding the dedication of trees.

www.ospreypublishing.com

Dedication
For Rainer Daehnhardt and the Sociedade Portuguesa de Armas Antiqs,
with thanks

Artist's Note
Readers may care to note that the original paintings from which the colour
plates in this book were prepared are available for private sale. All reproduction
copyright whatsoever is retained by the Publishers. All enquiries should be
addressed to:

www.gerryembleton.com
The Publishers regret that they can enter into no correspondence upon this
matter.

THE PORTUGUESE IN THE AGE OF DISCOVERIES c. 1340–1665

INTRODUCTION

St Ignatius of Loyola (1491–1556) in full armour, painted by an unknown Portuguese artist early in the 17th century. From the outset, Portuguese expeditions were motivated equally by the search for riches and military glory, and by missionary zeal. Loyola was a Portuguese knight; badly wounded by a cannonball in 1521, he discovered his calling while studying the scriptures during his long convalescence, and thereafter devoted his energies to the Church. In 1540 he founded the Society of Jesus, which sent Jesuit missionaries to Africa, India and the Far East. (Museu de S. Roque, Santa Casa de Misericordia de Lisboa, inv. 48, Lisbon)

Until the 15th century Portugal was a relatively isolated and unimportant country – thus its sudden emergence as a world power in the late 15th and 16th centuries seems particularly dramatic. This has led many historians to see Portugal's rise to maritime empire simply as the advance-guard of 'Western Civilization's' march to world dominance. In reality, the Portugal which led the way in terms of maritime expansion was still a Late Medieval rather than a Renaissance state; similarly, the first century of Portuguese expansion was more like a medieval Crusade than a Renaissance striving for enlightenment.

Not until the late 13th century did Portuguese become the official language of the state. Many years would also pass before Portuguese independence was accepted by its powerful neighbour, Castile. The struggle against Castilian domination did as much to forge Portuguese identity as did the thrust southwards against Islamic al-Andalus which was the Portuguese contribution to the supposedly 'Spanish' *Reconquista*. This anti-Islamic crusade took place at sea as well as on land. Islamic fleets attacked Lisbon several times during the 12th century, and Portuguese ships joined Frisian and Danish maritime crusaders to attack the Algarve region in 1189, where the more savage northerners slaughtered 6,000 Muslim prisoners. In 1217 King Afonso II of Portugal persuaded a largely German crusader fleet to support his attack on Alcacer do Sol. Within a few years the Algarve was conquered, with Silves finally falling in 1249.

The completion of the Portuguese Reconquista did not, of course, mean the end of significant Islamic influence in Portugal. In terms of maritime navigation, geographical knowledge and mapmaking, southern al-Andalus – including what was now southern Portugal – had been notably advanced during the later Islamic period, and such knowledge survived amongst the remaining Muslim and Jewish populations.

Until the 14th century Portugal remained a minor player in Atlantic navigation, despite being the heir to the naval heritage of Muslim Andalusian and North African mariners. The latter had defeated Viking fleets at sea on several occasions; they occasionally visited the Canary Islands, and knew the Cape Verde Islands, Madeira and probably the Azores. Substantial fishing fleets also operated out of Tangier and Ceuta, in the wake of earlier Andalusian ventures into the Atlantic.

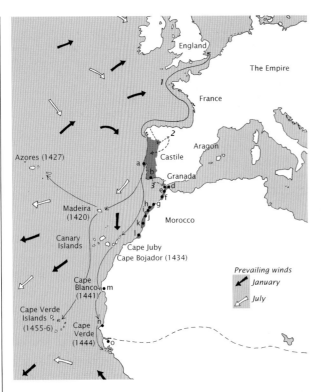

From the Hundred Years' War to the Age of Discoveries: Portuguese territory and outposts established before the death of Prince Henry the Navigator.
(1) Portuguese galleys operating in the English Channel as allies of England, 1380s.
(2) Anglo-Portuguese invasion of Castile, 1386–87.
(3) Portuguese invasion of northern Morocco – Ceuta, 1415; Tangier, captured 1437; Qasr al-Saghir, 1458.
(a) Lisbon; (b) Lagos; (c) Tangier; (d) Ceuta; (e) al-Qasr; (f) Arzilah; (g) Azamur; (h) Mazagão/ al-Jadidah; (i) Asafi; (j) Aguz/ Suwira'Adimah; (k) Agadir; (l) Massa; (m) Argiun; (n) Gorée; (o) Cacheu.

Islamic navigation around north-west Africa developed further during the 14th–15th centuries, as the Atlantic ports of Morocco increased in importance. Ships regularly traded as far as the mouth of the Wadi Sus (modern Agadir), but there seemed no reason to venture further, since Saharan caravan routes provided the necessary links. The coast south of the Wadi Draa was regarded as highly dangerous, and Islamic voyages south of Nūl Lamta (probably now Āzuqqī east of Cape Juby) remained hazardous and unprofitable – though this did not necessarily apply to less treacherous waters further out to sea.

The Portuguese were not much involved in the first struggles between Christian powers for domination over the trade of coastal Morocco and the Canary Islands, though some historians suggest that they were sailing further into the Atlantic, but keeping their discoveries to themselves. It has even been suggested that Portuguese explorers discovered Brazil during the 15th century, and in the mid-1470s the Portuguese ruler encouraged a voyage to Greenland, which had been known since Viking times – a voyage that may have pressed on to the coast of Canada. By the 15th century a realization that the world was spherical was generally accepted by educated Europeans, but Portugal's Islamic geographical heritage also included knowledge that Africa could be circumnavigated. Indeed, the idea that the wealth of India could be reached by sailing south was not new: an unsuccessful Genoese attempt had been made by the Vivaldi brothers in 1291. Then there was the lure of the Malian gold which, for centuries, Muslim merchants had brought across the Sahara: surely this could also be reached by sailing south?

Nevertheless, Portuguese commerce had previously looked eastwards into the Mediterranean, or northwards to the Low Countries and England, and the first recorded commercial treaty between Portugal and England was signed in 1294. Such commerce was sufficiently lucrative for Portugal and Castile to compete for domination of the sea routes around the Bay of Biscay, even before they found themselves supporting opposing sides during the Hundred Years' War between England and France.

Perhaps experience of these fearsome northern seas contributed to Portugal's only significant advantage over its future rivals in the Indian Ocean, which was in heavy ship design and marine artillery. But before reaching India the Portuguese had to work their way around Africa, establishing the outposts that were essential to maintaining regular commercial contacts over such vast distances. In medieval West Africa, Islamic expansion had as yet not reached much beyond Senegal and Guinea-Bissau. Several of the West African coastal peoples beyond this region had quite advanced civilizations, though their trade connections were with the interior, not the ocean. By contrast, East Africa had long

The main citadel of Fort Jesus at Mombasa in modern Kenya, as seen from the harbour. First captured in 1524, this site became one of the strongest and most important Portuguese fortresses along the East African coast. (Photo S. Pradines)

been linked to the wider world, and for centuries its long-distance commerce had been in the hands of Muslim merchants. The latter had gradually been pushing southwards, and had been established in the southern port of Sofala (near Beira, in modern Mozambique) since at least the 13th century. Since then other Muslim communities had established themselves far up the Zambezi valley, and further south at Bazaruto island. Meanwhile, the remarkably sophisticated Indian Ocean trading network was largely in the hands of Muslim Arabs, Persians, Arabized Africans, Muslim coastal communities from India, and, further east, Malay and Indonesian peoples who were still in the process of converting to Islam. For the Portuguese, all these would be regarded as 'Moors', and therefore hereditary enemies.

During the 14th century Islam had been on the defensive against the revived Christian Kingdom of Abyssinia (Ethiopia), which had invaded its smaller Muslim neighbours. Tales about this powerful Christian kingdom – inaccurate though they were, being centred on the legendary figure of 'Prester John' – would have a profound influence upon the first Portuguese explorers. Even before the Portuguese reached the Indian Ocean the discovery of entirely unknown peoples caused controversy in Europe, especially the 14th-century revelation of what were effectively 'Stone Age' inhabitants of the Canary Islands, almost on Europe's doorstep. This would be followed by contacts with the varied and often advanced cultures of sub-Saharan Africa, then the Neolithic tribal societies of Brazil, and the splendid imperial civilizations of the Aztecs, Incas and others. Many Europeans saw in these newly discovered 'primitive' peoples an innocent, idyllic way of life not far removed from that of Adam and Eve. (This essentially Medieval admiration would rapidly be replaced by an Early Modern realization that such peoples could be dominated, robbed, enslaved, expelled or even exterminated.)

Portuguese successes in the 16th century would inevitably encourage Spanish, English, Dutch and French competitors, but the Portuguese generally prevailed until

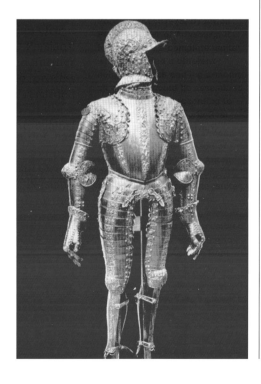

The decorated parade armour made for King Sebastião I of Portugal (r.1557–78) by Anton Pfeffenhauser of Augsburg. It forms part of a complete 'suite' which included a different helmet, cuirass and leg armour, all of which could be assembled in different ways according to military needs. (Armeria Real Madrid; photo A.F. Calvert)

5

almost 1600. Their greatest setback came, in fact, at the hands of their more traditional 'Moorish' rivals. The play known as *The Battell of Alcazar* was written by Shakespeare's less famous contemporary George Peele; its central event is the disaster that befell a Portuguese invasion of Morocco in 1578, though it focused upon the role played by one Captain Stukeley, an English Catholic who fought for the Portuguese. During the battle, the corpse of King Sebastião I is brought before his defeated ally, Abu Abdullah Muhammad:

(Enter two Portugals with the bodie of the king.)
Port. 'As gaue your grace in charge, right roiall prince,
The fields and sandie plaines we haue survaide,
And even among the thickest of his Lords,
The noble king of Portugall we found
Wrapt in his coulours coldly on the earth,
And done to death with many a mortall wound.'
Mahomet. 'Lo here my Lords, this is the earth and claie,
Of him that earst was mightie king of Portugall,
There let him lie, and you for this be free,
To make returne from hence to christendome.'

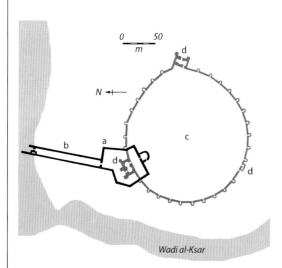

The fortified town of Qasr al-Saghir on the northern tip of Morocco was seized by the Portuguese in 1458. They then added a fort around the medieval 'Sea Gate', plus typical Andalusian long walls to the beach where ships could anchor. (a) Portuguese fort; (b) long walls to the 15th C shoreline; (c) medieval Islamic town surrounded by wall and towers; (d) medieval Islamic town gates. (After C.L. Redman, with additions by author)

0   50
m

N

Wadi al-Ksar

Sebastião's death did indeed prove catastrophic for Portugal. He left no son as heir, and King Philip II of Spain soon pressed his strong claim to the Portuguese throne. The resulting Spanish takeover in 1580, though legal, was widely resented, and was followed by what Portuguese historians usually call the 'Sixty Years' Captivity'. Portugal was dragged into Spain's disastrous naval confrontation with England; it then endured a 60-year struggle with its increasingly vigorous Dutch colonial rivals (1602–61) – which some have called the first real 'world war', for its vast geographical reach. In 1640 the Portuguese reclaimed their independence, resulting in a further long war, this time against Spain (1640–68). Although Portugal maintained much of its overseas empire, by the second half of the 17th century the country was in a state of exhaustion.

CHRONOLOGY

1250	Conquest of Faro from Muslims by King Afonso III completes the Portuguese *Reconquista*
1267	Castile abandons its claim to the Algarve (southern Portugal)
1344	Abortive crusade to Canary Islands planned
1385	Portuguese victories over Castile at battles of Trancoso and Aljubarrota secure Portuguese independence under King João I of Aviz (r.1385–1433)
1386	Anglo-Portuguese alliance agreed 'forever'
1415	Portuguese capture Ceuta in north-west Morocco
(1418–60)	(Vigorous Portuguese exploration of West African

	coast and South Atlantic under sponsorship of Prince Henry 'the Navigator')
1424	Attempted Portuguese settlement of Canary Islands
1434	Portuguese explore south of Cape Bojador on coast of Western Sahara
1437	Defeat of Portuguese attempt to conquer Tangier
1445	Portuguese settle in the Azores
1449	Internal struggles during childhood of King Afonso V (r.1438–81) end with his victory at Alfarrobeira
(1463–76)	(War with Morocco; Portuguese capture Tangier and Casablanca)
1474–76	Unsuccessful Portuguese intervention in Castilian dynastic struggle, ending with defeat by King Ferdinand of Aragon at battle of Toro
1481	Succession of King João II (r.1481–95), who revives programme of exploration. War between Portugal and Ottoman Empire
1488	Bartholomew Diaz sails round Cape of Good Hope from South Atlantic into Indian Ocean
1492	Capture of Granada completes the Spanish *Reconquista*
1494	Treaty of Tortesillas – Spain and Portugual agree respective zones of conquest in the Atlantic
1495	Succession of King Manuel I 'the Great' (r.1495–1521)
1498	Vasco da Gama reaches Malabar coast of south-west India
1500	Alvares Cabral lands in South America (Brazil). Portuguese fleet reaches Calicut on Malabar coast.
1500–05	Portugal establishes trading posts along west coast of India, the most important at Cochin (1503)
1505	Francisco de Almeida appointed first Viceroy of Portuguese India, and establishes trading outposts on East African coast
1507	*En route* to replace Almeida, Afonso de Albuquerque captures islands of Socotra and (briefly) Hormuz, commanding entrances to Red Sea and Persian Gulf respectively. Almeida's son Lorenzo establishes Portuguese settlement on Ceylon (Sri Lanka), and makes contact with sultanate of Malacca in East Indies (Indonesia).
1508	To resist Portuguese control of trade between Arab territories and India, the Muslim Sultan of Gujerat makes alliance with Mamluk Egypt; Lorenzo de Almeida is killed in action against their combined fleet. In December Albuquerque arrives at Cochin, but Almeida refuses to recognize his authority, and

The interior of the fort that the Portuguese added to the medieval Islamic fortified town of Qasr al-Saghir. (Author's photo)

	confines him while leading campaign to avenge his son's death.
1509	Almeida destroys ports along Indian west coast, including Goa and Dabul. In February, Almeida's victory over combined Muslim fleet and destruction of Diu will lead to Portuguese naval supremacy in the Persian Gulf and Red Sea, thus controlling north-western approaches to the Indian Ocean. Almeida hands over viceroyalty to Albuquerque. Portuguese trading post established at Malacca.
1510	Albuquerque seizes Goa, which becomes capital of the *Estado da Índia* (Indian Ocean empire)
1511	Albuquerque seizes Malacca, thus controlling eastern approaches to Indian Ocean
1512	Revolt at Goa, suppressed by Albuquerque on his return from Malacca
1513	Albuquerque's siege of Aden fails
1515	Albuquerque recaptures Hormuz, but is recalled to Portugal, and dies during the voyage
1519	Portuguese trading post established at Martaban, Burma
1529	Spanish and Portuguese agree zones of conquest in the Far East
(1529–43)	(Portuguese help Christian Ethiopia defeat invasion by the Ottoman Empire and Sultanate of Adal)
1536–37	Gujerat and Ottoman Empire form anti-Portuguese alliance. Viceroy da Cunha murders Sultan of Gujerat during parley.
(1538–63)	(Continuing Portuguese-Ottoman conflicts)
1538	Unsuccessful blockade of Diu by Ottoman fleet and Gujerati army
1542	Portuguese reach Japan
1557	Succession of King Sebastião I (r.1557–78). Portuguese establish trading base at Macau,

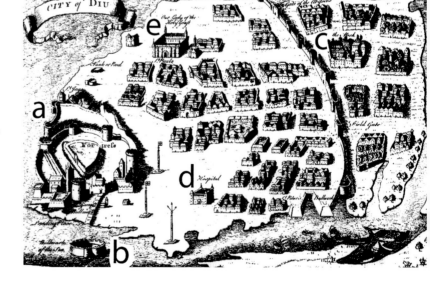

An English plan of the Portuguese trading city of Diu on the north-western coast of India, published in 1729 but showing the mid-16th century fortifications before they were modernized. (a) Fortress; (b) fortified islet called the Bulwark of the Sea; (c) fortified wall between inner and outer cities; (d) hospital; (e) cathedral of Our Lady of the Holy Ghost.

north-east China.

1559	Portuguese seize Daman, close to Diu
1566	Establishment of militia in Goa
1571	Portuguese establish colony in Angola, West Africa
1578	Portuguese defeated and King Sebastião killed at al-Qasr al-Kabir, Morocco
1580	After defeat of Dom Antonio de Crato by Duke of Alva at battle of Alcántara, King Philip II of Spain becomes King of Portugal
1580–89	Continuing Portuguese-Ottoman conflicts. De Crato fails in attempts to regain Portuguese independence, with help from French in 1582 and 1583, and from English in 1589.
1588	English defeat Spanish and Portuguese Armada
(1602–61)	(Conflicts between Dutch Republic and Portugal. Several trading bases on both sides of Atlantic change hands.)
1628	Portuguese overthrow Mwenemutapa Empire in Africa
1630	Creation of a *terço* 'regular company' in Goa
(1630–54)	(Dutch seize and hold part of Portuguese Brazil)
1640	Portugal reclaims independence under the Braganza dynasty, followed by Restoration War against Spain (1640–68)
1661	Portugal cedes Tangier and Mumbai (Bombay) to England
1662	Portuguese overthrow kingdom of Kongo in West Africa (roughly, modern northern Angola with parts of the two Congo republics)
1665	Victory at Montesclaros confirms Portuguese independence from Spain; Portugal regains its overseas empire except for Ceuta, which remains Spanish.

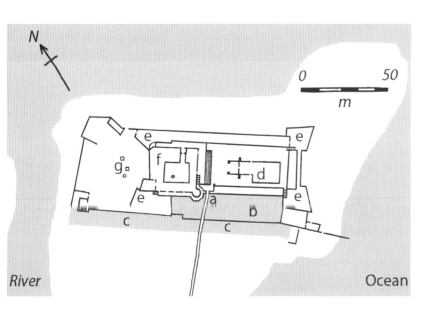

The fortress of the Portuguese trading post at São Jorge da Mina (now Elmina) on the coast of Ghana, as it appeared in September 1637. (a) Entrance; (b) rock-cut dry ditch; (c) rock-cut wet ditch; (d) church; (e) bastions; (f) late 15th C castle and governor's palace; (g) covered cistern with three draw-wells. (After A.W. Lawrence)

PORTUGUESE ARMIES BEFORE THE HUNDRED YEARS' WAR

During the 11th and 12th centuries a new aristocracy arose in Portugal, drawn from men who were rewarded for their roles during the Reconquista, including foreigners as well as locals. While *ricos-homens* families of higher rank were largely of foreign origin, those below them generally consisted of ancient free families of *ingenui*. Next came the *cavaleiros* cavalry, *escudeiros* squires and *infanções* infantry. By the 14th century there was also a clear division within the aristocracy, between those who lived close to the royal court and those who remained on their rural estates or *quintas* – which, in north-western Portugal, were often small and poor. Such 'knightly backwoodsmen' were the butt of satire, and, as in so many regions of feudal Europe, service at court offered the best hope of advancement for the younger or illegitimate sons of Portugal's rural aristocracy.

Until the military reforms of the later 14th century, military recruitment was based on an ancient system reflecting strong Andalusian influence. A 'goodman' class of land-owning farmers owning a horse, weapons and some armour were obliged to serve as *cavaleiros-vilãos* or 'peasant cavalry', and some of the urban merchant class also fell into this category. Free, property-owning peasants were expected to serve as *peões* infantry, though by the 14th century this term had largely lost its military meaning.

Portuguese armies continued to be organized along simple lines, largely based upon those of the earlier medieval kingdom of Asturias-León but also strongly influenced by Andalusian Islamic practice. The king was surrounded by a military household, while his leading vassals had their own smaller retinues. The *alférez* or ruler's standard-bearer was also the military commander. After working well until the mid-12th century, this system was then overhauled to face the Muwahhid-Islamic threat. This period also saw an increase in the number of castles held by the aristocracy and the Military Orders. Next came an attempt to impose a more hierarchical French-style feudal system upon the country, but this largely failed, because up to a tenth of the entire population seemed to claim some sort of aristocratic status; such families ranged from wealthy barons to poor families who had little more than an ancient name. Knights had served outside Portugal for decades, but this search for adventure intensified following the completion of Portugal's own Reconquista. Thus Portuguese often fought for Castile, as enthusiasm for the Crusade seemingly increased in 14th and 15th-century Portugal. On the other hand, Portuguese mercenaries also served the Muslim rulers of Morocco.

In tactical terms Portuguese armies were also distinct, but, as Portugal was by no means culturally isolated, the survival of seemingly archaic military practices probably reflected local circumstances. For example, the Portuguese Reconquista was completed before the full development of those light cavalry tactics *a la jinete* that characterized warfare between Granada and its Christian neighbours in the 14th and 15th centuries.

Pen and ink sketch of a knight, in a late 14th or early 15th-century Portuguese manuscript. (*Codice Alcobacense*, Ms. 208, f.32v, Biblioteca Nacional, Lisbon)

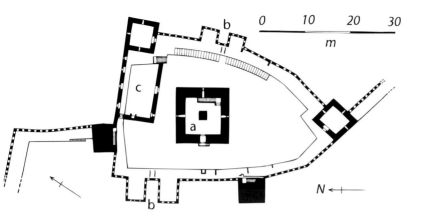

Guimarães in northern Portugal is called the cradle of the Portuguese nation. Its castle developed around a 10th century tower, and was greatly extended during the 15th century. (a) Early medieval keep; (b) gates; (c) hall. (After J.E. Kaufmann & H.W. Kaufmann)

Until the late 14th century Portuguese warfare clung to earlier Andalusian forms in which infantry played a major role, working in close co-operation with cavalry, and which paradoxically had much in common with the English styles of warfare during the Hundred Years' War.

The English alliance

Throughout most of the 14th century the main threat to Portugal's independence came from the crown of Castile, which, as the inheritor of earlier claims by León and Galicia, tended to see Portugal as a dependency. This tension lay behind an alliance between Portugal and England, which countered an alliance between France and one of the contending parties during a Castilian civil war. In 1380 England agreed to send an army of 3,000 'lances' and a similar number of archers to Portugal, under the Duke of Cambridge. This expedition achieved nothing, but it would be followed by others, including the English men-at-arms and archers who played a small but significant role in the decisive battle of Aljubarotta in 1385 – which also witnessed acombination of traditional Portuguese tactics with the new influence of Anglo-French warfare.

King Fernando I of Portugal was impressed by the effectiveness of English and French methods, soon insisting that his leading vassals field a certain number of men equipped in either the English or the French manner. The role of the *alférez mór* as overall commander beneath the king was abolished, replaced by the Anglo-French *marichal* (marshal) and *condestable* (constable), the latter being given greatly increased authority over the military aristocracy. Although old Arab-Andalusian terms for a battle array were replaced by Anglo-French terminology, the idea that it was Fernando who introduced a five-part array of centre, van, rear and wings is misleading; this had been standard practice in the Islamic parts of the Iberian peninsula since the 8th century.

The crossbow had long been used in Portuguese siege warfare. Now the Portuguese decided upon the training and enlistment of *besteiros* crossbowmen on a larger and more systematic scale, as a significant step towards the creation of a national army under royal control. The crossbowmen were mostly drawn from artisans, tradesmen and merchants rather than the retainers of the established aristocracy, while their weaponry was supplied by the royal administration. The new Aviz dynasty, which replaced the House of Afonso and ruled from 1385 to 1580, also

The barrel of a Spanish or Portuguese hand cannon, late 14th century. (Rainer Daehnhardt Collection, Lisbon)

recognized the importance of firearms, keeping guns and gunpowder under government control and setting up a central arsenal in Lisbon.

The Aviz dynasty succeeded in making direct royal vassals of a large proportion of Portugal's notoriously turbulent aristocracy of knights and squires, and these would provide most of the adventurous, warlike and ambitious manpower during Portugal's great period of overseas expansion. By the late 14th and early 15th centuries much of the country's elite already demonstrated an outward-looking mentality, as reflected in the popular chivalric *Tale of the Twelve Knights*. This described how 12 Portuguese heroes responded to a call to defend the honour of 12 English ladies who, feeling themselves insulted by 12 English knights, had complained to John of Gaunt, Duke of Lancaster, during his campaign in Portugal and northern Spain. (While 11 knights took ship from Porto to London, one insisted on travelling overland. The adventures of this Dom Alvaro Gonçalves Coutinho, nicknamed *O Magriço* or 'The Thin One', took him through Spain, Burgundy, France and Flanders. All the Portuguese knights won renown in this affair, while a letter from the Duke of Burgundy, supposedly dated 26 December 1411, is said to have thanked the Portuguese king for the sterling services done by *O Magriço*.)

ORGANIZATION & RECRUITMENT, c. 1400–1560

The fortified city of Evora, as it appeared in a Portuguese manuscript around 1504. (*Oficina regia de Lisboa*, Camera Municipal, Evora)

According to a Venetian intelligence report from the 1420s: 'The King of Portugal with all his revenues from clergy and laity, with all his force, would have, if he paid every month, at home 6,000 horsemen skilled in arms, abroad 3,000 horse. The King of Portugal had in 1410, 200,000 ducats revenue. By the wars it is reduced to 140,000 ducats'. This reliable source did not include semi-skilled militias – not that these were necessarily eager to serve. (For instance, in 1441 the Portuguese crown reportedly attempted to levy 14,000 men for a campaign in Morocco, but only 6,000 are said to have appeared.)

Like other European rulers, the Portuguese king largely relied upon professional forces, ranging from a Royal Guard of around 200 men in the mid-15th century, to the more numerous Military Orders. Not surprisingly, the crown wanted control over these quasi-religious organizations, and in 1420 the Pope finally allowed King João I's son, Prince Henry 'the Navigator', to be 'administrator' of the specifically Portuguese Order of Christ. Twenty-three years later this Order was granted 'spiritual administration and jurisdiction over all the coasts, islands and lands already conquered and yet to be conquered' – a major step in the creation of a Portuguese overseas empire.

During the 15th century, as Portuguese outposts spread down the West African coast, crusading motivation declined, but after the Portuguese rounded South Africa they almost immediately found themselves facing stiff Muslim resistance. This prompted a revival of hostility to Islam and of the prestige and wealth of the Military Order of Christ, and the militarization of the *armadas* – Portugal's exploration and trading fleets. Many leaders and captains joined the Order, and their fleets would sail from Lisbon beneath its banner. While the essentially medieval Military Orders retained their relevance for several centuries, other, more modern systems of overseas or 'imperial' administration developed, with Portuguese outposts being rated as *presidios* or *capitanias* ('captaincies') under commanders appointed by the crown. The result was a structure which, though built upon medieval feudal principles, proved remarkably effective until the later 16th century.

The completion of the Portuguese Reconquista, the peace with Castile and the end of Portugal's involvement in the Hundred Years' War had caused something of a crisis for a knightly class whose reason to exist was primarily military. Partly as a result of this, King João I of Portugal – like his contemporary King Henry V of England – needed a foreign war to keep his quarrelsome aristocracy occupied, and the chosen target was Sabta (Ceuta), on the Mediterranean coast of Morocco facing Gibraltar. North African adventures were only a partial solution, however, and many young men of high status sought adventure and spiritual and financial reward by joining those pirates who preyed upon Muslim shipping. Such men eventually formed a pool of belligerent manpower, skilled in maritime affairs, from whom Prince Henry the Navigator could recruit crews for longer-distance exploration.

Amongst the earliest of these adventurers was Lançarote de Freitas, who led two of the largest Portuguese expeditions down the West African coast in 1444 and 1446. He was described as a 'squire, brought up in the Infante's [Prince Henry's] house, an officer of the royal customs in the town of Lagos, and a man of great good sense'. Unfortunately for Lançarote's later reputation, the profits from his expeditions came largely from brutal slave-raiding.

From the mid-15th century onwards, the lower and middle-ranking leadership of Portuguese expeditions and of the resulting overseas outposts were the *fidalgos* – gentlemen descended from the old knightly class. The importance of such men was highlighted by Azurara (Gomes Eanes de Zurara) during the second half of the 15th century. His *Chronicle of the King Dom João I* described the force assembled to attack Ceuta, the most enthusiastic being younger men who 'ardently desired to acquire the merits of those who had given them life [their fathers], and following their example, to furnish proofs of courage and loyalty'.

Success led to a rapid expansion of a class known as the 'nobility of service', so that by the 16th century numerous *fidalgos* from minor and often poor aristocratic families would hang around the royal court, eager for a chance to show their worth. Consequently the Portuguese government was able to employ large numbers in its *armadas* and overseas captaincies, their exploits filling the 16th century chronicles and

Caricature of a nobleman sketched by an apparently bored clerk on a 15th-century Portuguese manuscript; despite its slightly exaggerated quality it provides valuably clear details of period costume. (*Cancioneiro da Ajuda*, Biblioteca da Ajuda, f. 231, Lisbon)

13

literature. For example, the greatest of Portuguese poets, Luís Vaz de Camões (1524–80), wrote an epic history of Portugal entitled *Os Lusiadas*, in which we read:

> The knights identified by their coats of arms
> Who left Portugal from our western beaches
> And sailing through seas never crossed before
> Went beyond Taprobana,[1]
> Faced dangers and overcame great wars
> Far beyond what was considered possible,
> And built among remote people
> A new kingdom they so highly honoured.

Followers of the *fidalgos*

Less is known about the ordinary soldiers and sailors, but during the 15th century every city, town and village in Portugal supposedly maintained up to 50 crossbowmen, ready for action. Other groups included 'gunsmiths of the king', 'crossbowmen of the royal council' and 'crossbowmen of the cavalry'. Those volunteers who fought in Morocco presumably included many such militiamen, and, clearly, some of those who went on early voyages to India and fought with such ferocity against Muslim foes in the Indian Ocean had honed their skills against the Muslims of North Africa.

Infantry spearmen preceding fully armoured cavalry, in a tapestry illustrating the assault on Asilah in 1471 during King Afonso V's invasion of northern Morocco. The nearest horseman wears a salet helmet with a plume, a fluted or corrugated skull and large gilded rivets; note also his laminated plate upper-arm defences. (Facsimile of Pastrana Tapestries, Segovia Castle Museum; author's photo)

Needless to add, the reality of a new life overseas was not always as attractive as the settlers hoped. One of the lesser-known attempts at colonization was in Canada, where João Alvares Fagundas attempted Portugal's only North Atlantic colony. Some time after 1521 he assembled volunteers from north-western Portugal and the Azores, and established a settlement named São João on what is now Cape Breton Island. Faced with hostility from the indigenous American tribes and from French fishermen, most of the colonists went home in 1525.

As opportunities for easy profit became fewer and the numbers of volunteers declined, the Portuguese legal system offered an alternative supply of manpower. Service in the galleys had been used as a punishment during the 15th century, but was now increasingly replaced by sending men into enforced exile in various colonial outposts. These were the *degredados*, usually unmarried men picked up for various misdemeanours in periodic sweeps of the country. Although (surprisingly) the system was only supposed to apply to the aristocracy, it soon caught up all ranks of society, with

---

1 Either Sri Lanka, Sumatra, or an entirely mythical island in the Indian Ocean.

those lower down the scale tending to be shipped furthest away. Once at their destination, however, the *degredados* were free to move around – though not to leave – and in 1534 King Dom João III issued a law that banned the beating of *degredados*, stating that they should be treated in the same manner as everyone else. In practice it was virtually impossible to separate enforced *degredados* from volunteers, when both had essentially the same military duties and both were paid, and in Brazil *degredados* held many important positions by the mid-16th century.

Portuguese Brazil had an 'open frontier' to the wilderness, beyond which escaped *degredados* could live independently among relatively primitive tribal peoples outside Portuguese control. However, escaping from an outpost in India entailed the refugee being accepted as a renegade within one of the neighbouring Islamic or Hindu states, and fleeing from an African outpost is likely to have been even more hazardous. Those convicted of more serious crimes, and referred to as *lançados*, were simply dumped on the African coast, where those who survived served as intermediaries between local populations and the nearest Portuguese authorities. Not suprisingly, they or their descendants soon 'went native', and formed the foundation of subsequent mixed-race communities.

Another scene from the Pastrana Tapestries, showing one of the riders on an armoured horse. Note also the careful depiction of infantry spearmen protected by a combination of brigandines, mail and plate armour; the sleeved brigandines are an unusual feature. (Segovia Castle Museum; author's photo)

Meanwhile, the very lengthy voyages from Portugal to its colonial outposts took a heavy toll. In the 16th century a typical large outward-bound trans-oceanic ship – *não da carreira da India*, 'ship for the passage to India' – had a crew of about 120 and carried as many as 400 to 500 passengers, almost entirely volunteers and *degredados*. The Portuguese authorities preferred such journeys to be completed non-stop to avoid opportunities for desertion, but in fact this was rarely possible; most convoys had to make one or more stops at designated *escalas* (defended ports) during the voyage.

Whereas the leaders of the earliest voyages of discovery were, where possible, drawn from men with experience of the seas, the captaincy of individual ships and appointment as *capitão-mor* – the commander of the *armadas* or annual fleets to India – were gifts of the crown. As such, they were usually given to noblemen or their closest followers, as a potentially profitable reward for good service. Although the government tried to ensure that the commander had some maritime experience, in the words of one observer the job might go to a *fidalgo* who 'had never seen any water other than the River Tagus'. Therefore, the contribution of experienced but lower-ranking pilots remained essential – but such men were few in number. Their task demanded long experience, but casualties were high because of disease,

Infantry arquebusiers and artillery during Dom João de Castro's triumphal entry into Goa in 1538, depicted in a sequence of tapestries made in Flanders in *c.*1560 to celebrate Dom João's career as *Vice-rei da Índia*. (Museu Nacional de Arte Antiga, Lisbon)

accident and conflict during the long voyages to India, and it was not unknown for early 16th-century fleets to set sail from Lisbon with crews made up almost entirely of raw land-lubbers.

Losses from disease and battle meant that there were in fact never more than about 10,000 able-bodied Europeans and local Eurasians available for naval and military service in Portugal's territories between East Africa and the Far East. These included a Goan militia, established in 1566 'for emergencies only'. Furthermore, it was rare for more than 1,000 reinforcements to be sent from Portugal even in emergencies. Consequently, a few hundred *soldados* or unmarried men receiving pay remained the basis of the Portuguese military presence in Goa. (The *morador* settler usually had the status of *casado* or married man.) At other times Goa might be home to 5,000 'idle', unpaid soldiers during the rainy season when there could be no campaigning.

Loose organization

During the 16th and most of the 17th century, Portuguese military organization in India was hardly more sophisticated than that of their Indian rivals. This was most obvious amongst the infantry, there being no real 'regiments' of footsoldiers before the 18th century. Instead, Portuguese soldiers – whether volunteers or *degredados* – simply signed up with their chosen *fidalgo*, often receiving little training, no uniforms and no standardized weaponry. In India this was done at the start of the campaigning season, at the end of the monsoon rains in autumn. The resulting 'companies' would disband at the end of that season, usually when the monsoon returned in May or June. Once their pay was spent, the soldiers were often left to beg for their sustenance in the streets of Goa until recruiting started again.

The limitations of this system were obvious, and were a major reason for the fiscal reforms that Viceroy Linhares of Goa tried to introduce in 1630. The Hapsburg rulers of Spain and Portugal had long wished to remodel the Portuguese army along Spanish lines, but had backed down in the face of fierce opposition from the established military elite of *fidalgos*. Linhares informed the local council that he planned to establish a *terço* unit of 2,500 permanently paid soldiers, in addition to the 5,000-strong militia. Despite considerable hostility, around 900 men had signed up by June 1631, and Linhares issued the new regiment with a comprehensive *regimento* or set of rules. Nevertheless further recruitment faltered, and, despite encouragement from Lisbon, Linhares failed to save his new infantry *terço*, which had ceased to exist by late 1634 (though it would later be revived and strengthened).

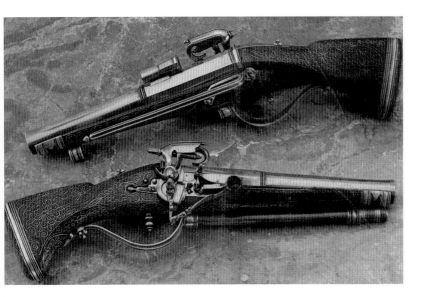

MERCENARIES & COLONIAL FORCES

Portuguese 'soldiers of fortune' living outside Portuguese territory eventually outnumbered the official garrisons, and, although most were mercenaries rather than renegades, many seem to have been deserters. They included Eurasians as well as Europeans, all being Portuguese in culture. One reason why a soldier might desert was the fact that a European had to serve for ten years before being allowed back to Portugal. Efforts were made to shorten this period of mandatory service, though conditions always seem to have been added (such as marrying one of the orphan girls who had been sent out to Goa).

The years between 1570 and 1610 were the high-water mark of such Portuguese mercenaries, who were often numerous enough to form freebooting companies under elected leaders. Those who fled from the Portuguese enclaves after committing crimes may not have been particularly missed, but when fully-trained soldiers deserted to a Muslim ruler this was considered very serious. The largest numbers of such *renegados*, as they were called, fought for the Mughul Emperors of India, and as a result a substantial Portuguese community was established in Agra, the Mughul capital, during the 16th century. Even as early as 1503 two Italian gunners from Milan deserted Portuguese service to enter that of the Hindu Samoothiris. Other *renegados* also fought for the Hindu kingdom of Vijayanagar until its destruction in 1565, while the garrison of Asirgarh fortress in the Deccan are known to have included Portuguese artillery officers who had converted to Islam.

The crusading character of the earliest Portuguese overseas campaigns meant that they attracted religiously motivated foreign volunteers. According to Azurara, for example, two squires from south-western France 'who had rendered the king great service in the [previous] war' wanted to join Prince Henry the Navigator's attack on Ceuta in 1415. Other foreigner volunteers included

The fortified tower built by the Portuguese on a rocky islet facing Qurayat, on the coast of Oman. (Author's photo)

noblemen and 'merchant adventurers' from England and Germany, the latter including a 'German gentleman' who fought alongside Ruy Gonçalves during the assault upon Ceuta. By the 16th century skilled gunners were much more welcome than wandering noblemen, and many Venetian, German and Flemish gunners served in the East – both for and against the Portuguese. For example, in 1525 the Portuguese authorities in Cochin informed Lisbon that 'There is a great need for a hundred gunners, half of them Germans, and the remainder Portuguese, and better trained in their profession than those who have come out here in recent years'. The Portuguese army that was defeated at al-Qasr al-Kabir in 1578 included a professional Castilian force of 2,000, but also numerous foreign volunteers and mercenaries including Italian and Irish Roman Catholics, as well as a few unexpected Dutch and German Protestants.

European prisoners-of-war could also find themselves fighting for Portugal, and the story of the English sailor Andrew Battell is a case in point. He was captured in Brazil by local tribesmen, who sold him to the Portuguese; they in turn shipped the Englishman to Angola in West Africa, where he was sent up river to join the garrison of a fort. When the resident pilot of this outpost died, Battell, as a skilled seaman, was entrusted with sailing the governor's ship back to Luanda. Next he was sent to the River Congo (Zaire) with a trading mission. Having tried and failed to escape in a Dutch ship, Battell was banished inland, and spent the following six years as part of the Portuguese garrison at Massangano. Further adventures followed, until, as a reward for loyal service and being a good shot, Battell was made 'a sergeant in the Portugal company'. Eventually this remarkable man returned to England, and settled at Leigh-on-Sea in Essex.

Local recruitment

During the early decades of Portuguese overseas conquests there was virtually no use of colonial or indigenous troops. Nevertheless, Gonçalo Velho Cabral reportedly left 'a few Moors' (of uncertain origin) on the uninhabited Azores islands in May 1444, with instructions to explore the country before he returned the following spring with some European settlers. Since Madeira and the Azores had been uninhabited, there was no mixing of settler and native peoples. In Africa, mixed-blood communities soon appeared; unavoidably, the names given to them are often offensive to modern ears, but at the time they were merely descriptive – the most common being *mulatto*. In fact, the West African *mulatto* community soon played a vital role as intermediaries between the Portuguese and their African neighbours.

One of the first Portuguese colonial forces was raised in 1535 to deal with a specific threat – that of escaped slaves on the island of São Tomé. These desperate people, unable to reach the African mainland, formed themselves into armed bands which terrorized the Portuguese settlers. Eventually the local authorities asked for royal permission and money to organize a local force to attack the fortified *mocambo* settlements of the escaped slaves.

The problem of insufficient local troops persisted in most Portuguese African territories during the 16th and 17th centuries, and it came to a head in Angola when the King of Kongo allied himself with the Dutch enemy. In this desperate situation a substantial force of 650 men was shipped over from Brazil in 1665, while others were sent from the separate Portuguese captaincy of Pernambuco. These South Americans joined forces with the Portuguese garrison troops, who were also supported by local African soldiers known as *empacaseiros* (from *mpakasa*, 'buffalo-hunter'). One of the most successful leaders during this war was a *mulatto* named Luís Lopés de Sequeira, and within two

decades the Portuguese authorities finally agreed that no distinction be made between 'whites, *mulattos* and free negroes' serving in Angolan garrisons – henceforward, promotion would be on merit alone.

In East Africa there had also been settlement of some areas beyond the control and protection of Portuguese coastal garrisons. These *sertanejo* backwoodsmen included *degredados*, escaped criminals, and even a few members of the aristocracy, all apparently unwilling to accept the discipline of fortress and garrison life. While the government had sufficient troops to control the coastal strip, settlement and the establishment of 'commercial fairs' for trade deeper in the interior forced the authorities to rely on the armed followers of the most powerful settler *senhores*, each of whom had his *bandazio*. These local strongmen were indispensable, but less easy for the government to control – indeed, powerful private armies were soon forcing land concessions from the local African chiefs. An armed retainer of an Afro- Portuguese *senhor* was called a *chicunda*, literally 'slave', serving in an *ensaca* or company.

Although Portugal controlled relatively little territory in Asia, with the exception of a brief domination of the island of Sri Lanka, these lands had substantial mixed populations in the *aldeia* tax districts granted to *fidalgos*, and among these communities loyalty to Portugal and to Catholic Christianity became very strong. The most important outpost was Goa, where, as in Portugal's other Indian enclaves, those estates with military obligations were known as *aforamentos*. Their inhabitants' main duty was to maintain a cavalry horse; unfortunately the system did not always work, especially when the Church took over land and thereby removed their military obligations. In 1614, for example, an enquiry found that many villages in the coastal enclave of Damão (Daman) had been improperly leased without their military obligations being enforced. Five years later only six or seven of the 60 around the fort of Baçaim (Bassein) that were obliged to maintain horses under the terms of their *aforamentos* were currently doing so.

The Portuguese fleeing during the Mughul conquest of Hugli, north-east of Calcutta, in 1632. The artist who illustrated the *Padshahnama* Mughul manuscript may not have known much about European ships, but his representation of the Portuguese and their local allies was remarkably accurate. (Royal Collection, inv. no. 1005025, London)

19

In Brazil, the first colonial troops were auxiliaries, militias, or temporary members of *bandeiras* armed columns (literally, 'flags') – which initially were little more than slave-raiding exeditions against local tribes. As in so many other parts of the world, such raiders were frequently supported by the tribal enemies of those they targeted. The *bandeirantes* themselves were organized as quasi-military companies within the frontier zones of Brazil, and while some of their expeditions were officially sanctioned, most were not. Instead, a number of individuals agreed to follow a recognized leader in pursuit of profit – usually in the form of slaves. The resulting *bandeiras* were invariably multi-ethnic, and the small number of Europeans did not necessarily provide the leadership. This normally went to the most experienced man available, often a *mameluco* of mixed European-Amerindian origin who spoke the local language.

These unsavoury raiding bands nevertheless stood Brazil in good stead in 1630, when it was suddenly invaded by the Dutch. The Luso-Brazilian (Brazilian Portuguese) defending forces were probably more multi-racial than any other army in the world at that time, including Europeans, Amerindians, blacks, *mulattos,* and people described as 'half-breeds of various kinds'. Their effectiveness came as a shock to the very consciously white Dutch troops. Amongst the most notable Portuguese field commanders were Camarão, a 'full-blooded Amerindian chief', and Henrique Dias, a 'full-blooded Negro'. For his role in a black military unit at Pernambuco, Dias was awarded a *foro de fidalgo* or patent of nobility by King Philip IV in 1633. Five years later he was knighted as a member of a Military Order with a stipend of 40 *escudos* (high value coin) a month, though the authorities in Brazil apparently baulked at funding such royal generosity. Several of Henrique Dias' colleagues in the black *terço* also faced the same problems, though three others were eventually raised to noble rank.

A mid-17th century French engraving showing a Portuguese military drummer in 1639, when Goa was blockaded but not taken by a Dutch fleet. (Anne S.K. Brown Military Collection, Brown University Library, Providence; photo R. Chartrand)

MOTIVATION, TRAINING & MORALE

There was at first little public support for Prince Henry the Navigator's dreams of exploration, largely because few saw any profit in it, but these attitudes rapidly changed when wealth began to flow into Portugal, and the aristocratic elite recognized the opportunities for honour and adventure as well as profit. The first area to benefit was the Algarve, and especially the port of Lagos. According to Azurara, 'people of this area were therefore the first to ask the Infante [Prince Henry] for leave to go to the countries whence these Moors [the first black slaves] were brought, for no ship could go thither without the special permission of the Infante'.

The first victims of Portuguese slave-raiding included both Muslims and black Africans. The Ceuta operation in 1415 was reportedly provoked by Muslim slave-raiding on the coast of Portugal, and subjecting their people to the same treatment was seen as a continuation of the fundamentally anti-Islamic and anti-Jewish Reconquista. Religious motivation remained a major factor, and the Portuguese forces that seized various other coastal enclaves in Morocco during the 15th century saw themselves as crusaders. Even as late as 1578 King Sebastião I – killed that year at the battle of al-Qasr al-Kabir – was motivated by somewhat outdated crusading ideals. Earlier in that century the orders given to Pedro Álvares Cabral, commander of an *armada* sailing to the East, clearly reflected a fundamental hostility to Islam: 'If you encounter ships belonging to the aforesaid Moors of Mecca at sea, you must endeavour as much as you can to take possession of them, and of their merchandise and property and also of the Moors who are in the ships, to your profit as best you can, and to make war upon them and do as much damage as possible to a people with whom we have so great and so ancient an enmity'.

Portuguese ferocity demoralized many of their foes for decades (as when some Muslim soldiers aboard a ship at Diu, India, threw themselves into the sea in full armour rather than be captured). While the Portuguese frequently mutilated Muslim captives they hardly ever treated Hindus so harshly. Meanwhile, the continuing spread of Islam horrified Portuguese missionaries because they knew it was practically impossible to convert Muslims, though they remained more hopeful where 'heathen' Hindus and Buddhists were concerned. (One of the most interesting aspects of the initial Portuguese encounter with Hinduism was a belief that Hindus were heretical Christians who might be brought back to the 'true Catholic path'.) Non-Christian practices were banned during the early decades of the Portuguese presence in India, and in 1567 an official decree attempted to end all socializing between Portuguese families and their non-Christian neighbours. In reality such contacts increased; apart from anything else, dancing girls and temple prostitutes in neighbouring Hindu territory proved highly popular with many Portuguese *fidalgos*.

In West Africa the Portuguese conversion of the King of Kongo, best known by his new Christian name of Afonso I (1506–43), proved to be a significant event, since many of his aristocracy followed suit. However, a resulting centralization of power in this kingdom led to increased warfare, slave-trading, and refugee population movements.

One of Portugal's most significant failures in its efforts to spread Catholic Christianity was in Ethiopia. Here the official religion of the state, though not necessarily of the majority of its subjects, was already Christian. The goodwill generated by Portuguese assistance during the defeat of Ahmad Gragn's Islamic invasion was destroyed by the heavy-handed behaviour of Jesuit missionaries. As a consequence, King Fasilades of Ethiopia (r.1632–1667) expelled the Jesuits and restored the kingdom's traditional Monophysite Church, whose religious links were with the Coptic Patriarchate of Egypt rather than the Papacy in Rome. The Ethiopians even formed a semi-official alliance with the Ottoman Turks against future Portuguese attempts to dominate them.

The Reformation had already divided Western European Christendom between Protestants and Catholics, and this had a direct military impact upon Portugal's overseas territories, with the Portuguese complaining that English 'heretics' supplied the Muslim Moroccans with firearms and gunpowder. Half a century later, the 17th-century struggle between Catholic Portuguese and Protestant Dutch resulted in what has been described as the Portuguese Order of Christ's 'last hurrah'. Indeed, the struggle between Catholics and Protestants loomed so large in people's

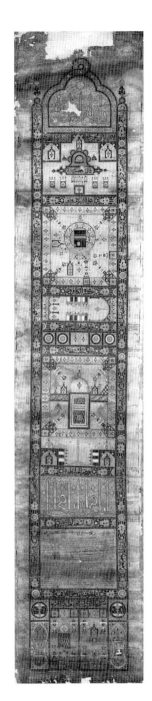

A Muslim Hajj certificate which includes a Portuguese translation of the Arabic text. Dating from the 16th century, this proof that a surrogate pilgrim went to Mecca and Medina was made either for a Portuguese-speaking Muslim living somewhere in the Portuguese empire, or even for a Portuguese convert to Islam. (Kongelike Bibliotek, Cod. Arab. Add. 087, Copenhagen)

Christ and the Centurion, a panel painting by the school of Jorge Afonso, c.1510–15, in which the Roman officer and his followers appear as typical members of the early 16th-century Portuguese military elite. (Charola do convento de Cristo, Tomar)

minds that it may have contributed to the muted Portuguese response to their throne being taken over by a Spanish king in 1580.

Other, more personal motivations were apparent throughout these centuries. Amongst the strongest was a desire for military or chivalric fame, which was deep-seated within the Portuguese military elite. One of their most popular heroes was Nuno Álvares Pereira, who served as Constable during the epic 14th-century struggle against Castile. Born illegitimate, though of a noble family, he was sent to court at the age of 13, becoming a seemingly invincible warrior and something of a religious mystic. Despite wanting to remain celibate he bowed to his mother's wishes that he marry, but never consumated the union.

The 'chivalry' displayed by the fleet assembled to attack Ceuta in 1415 was rather more material. According to Azurara: 'Dom Henrique [Prince Henry] did not forget to have magnificent liveries made for all his captains; and those lords in their turn clad their men in the colours of their houses'. Similarly, 'All the ships of war, galleys and other vessels were adorned with the great standards of the Knights of Christ and little flags with the colours and the device of the Infante [Prince Henry]; and as they were new and richly adorned with gold, men marvelled to behold them'. At the same time, 'to the contrary of what might have been believed, the persons of high rank wore the liveries of woollen, and those of lower rank the silken garments'.

The medieval habit of dubbing deserving men as knights on the battlefield continued during the Portuguese conquests of the 15th and 16th centuries. Hope of such advancement clearly motivated many volunteers, who showed their service records at court when requesting *doações* (donations) – modest land grants close to one of the fortified overseas outposts. The *mouros de paz* or native inhabitants of theoretically pacified villages on such land then paid tax which was given to the captain of the nearby fort. In practice this system never really worked, and those seeking a reward or favour usually looked for land within Portugal or in genuinely pacified territories.

For those lower down the social scale the primary motivations remained religious and financial, as recorded by Azurara after the conquest of Ceuta: 'The King … also gave great largesse to those of the common people who had done well, each according to his trade. And all were content'. The hope of profit loomed large during the great exploratory voyages of the late 15th and early 16th centuries, even when there seems to have been no very clear agreement about pay, and in practice the survivors of such a royally licensed *entrada* could expect generous rewards once they got home. On other occasions financial terms were agreed beforehand. Writing about Cabral's great voyage, Gaspar Correa stated that 'The chief captain of the fleet should have for the voyage 10,000 *cruzados* [gold coins] and 500 quintals [units of weight approximately equal to 100lb] of pepper, paid for from his salary of 10,000 *cruzados* at the price at which the king might purchase it…; and to the masters and pilots 500 *cruzados* for the voyage and 30 quintals of pepper and four chests free; and to the captains of the ships 1,000 *cruzados* for each 100 tons, and six chests free, and 50 quintals of pepper…'. (In the early days of exploration and spice-trading, pepper was worth roughly its own weight in gold in Europe.)

Training

The little that is known about Portuguese military training comes from specialist works, such as the *Livro Da Ensinança De Bem Cavalagar Todo Sela* ('The art of riding in every saddle') written by King Duarte in 1438 (see 'Select Bibliography', Dom Duarte, *The Royal Book of Jousting…*). When considering how to use a spear on horseback it describes four methods, but notes that skill in throwing a spear as a javelin must first be learned on foot. This was an essentially Moorish-Andalusian tactic, which entailed the use of a different saddle:

> …he should be riding a horse with a *Gineta [jinete]* saddle and short stirrup straps, carrying the spear … with the arm relaxed and loose; then, he gets his horse to a steady gallop … with the wind coming from behind, and not touching the horse's bridle until he throws the spear… Doing it this way, he should be able to throw the spear exceeding at least by one-third the distance he normally reaches when he throws it on foot.

King Duarte's advice on the use of the sword similarly reflects residual Islamic influence rather then repeating the fencing techniques seen in most other parts of Western Europe. The king advised that Portuguese cavalrymen should become skilled in all styles of riding, thus achieving greater military flexibility than horsemen from Morocco, who were unable to ride properly in a *Bramanta* saddle (the deep Western European form with long stirrup leathers), or Englishmen or Frenchmen, who were unused to the shallow Moroccan *jinete* saddle with short stirrups.

In the 17th century one of the few military advantages that the Portuguese enjoyed during their long struggle against the Dutch was their generally greater acclimatization to the tropics. Their troops also displayed notably greater skill in what might be called bush warfare, against an enemy whose military experience had largely been on the cooler and more organized battlefields of northern Europe.

Morale

The high morale demonstrated by so many Portuguese *fidalgos* and ordinary soldiers during the Age of Discoveries astonished friends, foes and neutrals alike. Wounds came to be seen as marks of distinction, at least in the eyes of chroniclers like Couto. Describing a skirmish with local forces in Sri Lanka, he wrote of one of the wounded Portuguese that 'a good deal of blood ran down his fine long beard, which made him an even handsomer and more noble-looking gentleman'.

Ruy Freyre d'Andrade might be seen as an example of the generous but also capricious *fidalgo* of this period. For instance, in 1614, while serving as the captain of Chaul south of Mumbai, he was wounded in the belly by a musket ball. This terrified his outnumbered troops, but despite the seriousness of his injury d'Andrade rallied them and conducted a retirement in good order. During these campaigns Ruy

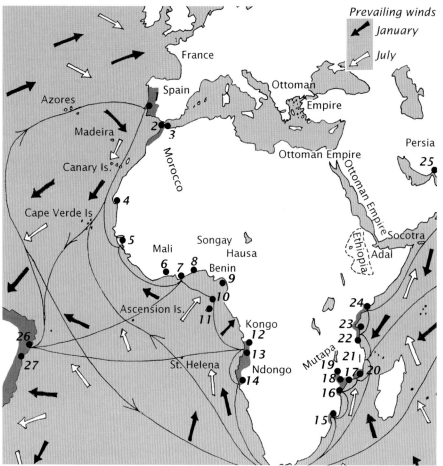

Portuguese outposts in Africa, mid-15th to mid-17th C, and main trade routes.
(1) Lisbon; (2) Tangier; (3) Ceuta;
(4) Argiun; (5) Cacheu; (6) Axim;
(7) Elmina; (8) Accra;
(9) Fernando Po; (10) Principe
Island; (11) São Tomé;
(12) Ambriz; (13) Luanda;
(14) Benguela; (15) Delagoa;
(16) Sofala; (17) Quelimane;
(18) Sena; (19) Tete;
(20) Mozambique; (21) Querimba
Island; (22) Kilwe; (23) – Zanzibar;
(24) Mombasa; (25) Hormuz.
Brazil:(26) Recife;
(27) Salvadorde Bahia.

Freyre d'Andrade also kept open house for the poorer soldiers. The Ethiopian *Royal Chronicles* at the time of King Gelawdewos (1521–59) described the Portuguese as being 'powerful and valorous men, athirst for war like wolves and hungry for the fight like lions'. The Chinese were less impressed, describing the Portuguese as a particularly warlike and uncivilized type of 'southern barbarian' – that being the direction from which the first Portuguese ships arrived.

High morale was maintained until the later 16th century, and, despite increasing casualties, Portuguese dominance still appeared unassailable in 1580. The fact that many Portuguese residents in the East already looked upon India as their homeland would be a potent source of strength in the forthcoming struggle against the Dutch. Unfortunately, the ordinary soldiers were not so happy, and even in the 16th century the playwright Ferreira de Vasconcelos had a veteran grumbling that 'The hospitals are full of loyal fools'. This disenchantment was similarly reflected in a verse by Manuel de Faris e Sousa, written in 1627:

'Heroic Lusitania…
Who has been able to shine so brightly in the wars,
You have tarnished your glory
Within the bounds of Ceres and Tethys's foamy realm
When you refused to honour sword or pen'.

Indeed, complaints by old soldiers who felt poorly rewarded would become a recurring theme in 17th-century Portuguese literature; Camões complained that 'we see stout-hearted men fall to a low estate, humble, obscure, ending their lives in wretched pauper's beds'. Even down- to-earth commentators like Couto bemoaned the fact that while great rewards went to leaders, the common soldiers failed to get their fair share.

(continued on page 33)

PORTUGAL, c.1340s–80s
1: Sergeant, c.1340s–80s
2: Knight, c.1340s–50s
3: Knight, c.1370s–80s

A

CANARY ISLANDS, EARLY 15th CENTURY
1: Knight
2: Hand-gunner
3: Scribe
4: Guanche native

EXPLORATION & SLAVE-RAIDING, MID 15th CENTURY
1: Commander
2: Crossbowman
3: Sailor

C

INVASION OF MOROCCO, LATE 15th
CENTURY
1: Man-at-arms
2: Infantryman
3: Standard-bearer

D

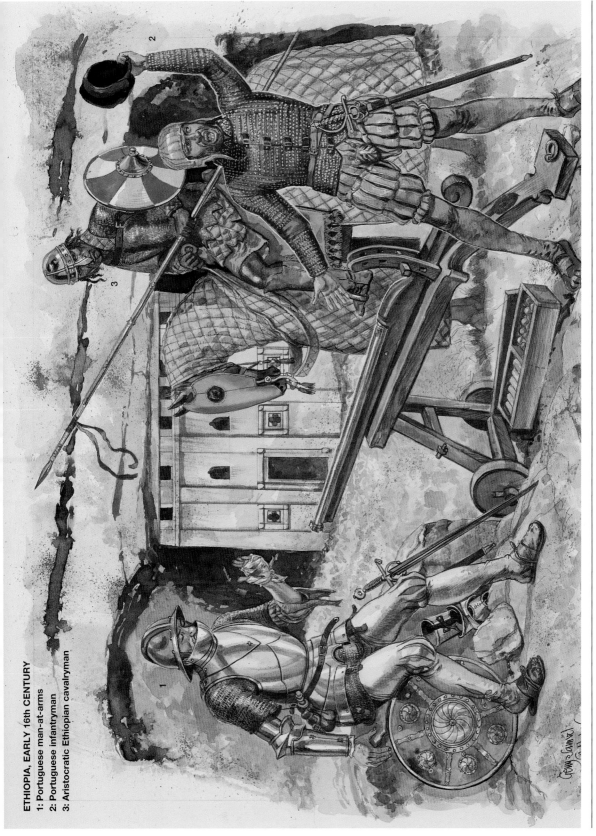

ETHIOPIA, EARLY 16th CENTURY
1: Portuguese man-at-arms
2: Portuguese infantryman
3: Aristocratic Ethiopian cavalryman

E

BRAZIL, 16th CENTURY
1: Brazilian Tupinamba chief
2: Brazilian-Portuguese nobleman, c.1550s
3: Afro-Brazilian retainer, c.1580s

F

INDIAN OCEAN, LATE 16th–EARLY 17th CENTURY
1: Goan-Indian soldier in Portuguese service
2: Portuguese man-at-arms
3: Portuguese soldier, c.1580s–90s

SOUTHERN AFRICA, c.1600–1650
1: Portuguese soldier
2: African warrior in Portuguese service
3: Portuguese officer, c.1650

H

STRATEGY & TACTICS

The strategy of Portuguese expansion developed during the 16th century, but one overriding feature remained – the extremely scattered nature of most Portuguese outposts. Since their 'empire' really consisted only of interlinked chains of ports along various sea lanes, it did not take them long to realize that their scattered possessions around the Indian Ocean could not be governed effectively from one centre, so in 1509 a separate governor-general was appointed for the enclaves in Africa and Arabia.

Portuguese confidence was neverthleless riding high, and shortly before his death in 1515 Afonso de Albuquerque, the brilliant admiral who was the chief architect of Portuguese India, proudly informed his king that 'I leave the chief places in India in Your Majesty's power … the only thing left to be done being the closing of the gates of the [Bab al-Mandib] straits' at the southern end of the Red Sea. He had earlier maintained that Portugal's eastern empire could be built around 'four good fortresses and a large, well-armed fleet manned by 3,000 European-born Portuguese'. In the event only three of Albuquerque's four targets were taken – Goa, Malacca and Hormuz – while Aden eluded the Portuguese grasp. There also seems to have been only one occasion when Portugal raised such a substantial fleet – that sent to relieve Malacca in 1606. Nevertheless, fortified coastal and trading posts known as *feitorias* soon stretched from Sofala in south-east Africa to Ternate in the Moluccas. Another wave of conquests followed during the late 16th and early 17th centuries, though the subsequent prolonged war with the Dutch forced the Portuguese onto the defensive.

Meanwhile, Portuguese ambitions in north-west Africa were drastically cut back. Whereas some 200 ships and 8,000 men had been sent in 1515 to take São Joao da Mamora (now Mahdiya on the Atlantic coast of Morocco), and eight garrisons with a nominal total of 5,000 troops were still maintained in 1542, the scale of Portugal's committment was reduced to a more manageable level during the second half of the 16th century.

Several centuries passed before the original 'fort system', by which Portuguese control in West Africa was confined to tiny coastal enclaves, evolved into true colonies. However, early in the 16th century, Portugal had already decided to treat the south-west African state of Ndongo, south of the powerful kingdom of Kongo, as a conquest rather than as an ally or tributary. Initially the Portuguese built and garrisoned a fortress to protect a small band of settlers in the normal way, but they then gradually imposed their control over nearby peoples. By the late 16th century some local chieftains had become Portugal's allies, their warriors helping the Portuguese expand across what became Angola.

Portuguese military activity in 16th-century Angola responded to the movement of peoples who were themselves reacting to internal African warfare, slave-raiding, and periodic droughts. When Portuguese *pombeiro* trading caravans were attacked the Portuguese responded in kind, though this sporadic warfare rarely had much lasting impact upon either side. Even the establishment of Portuguese rule over a substantial part of the country between 1610 and 1620 was a reaction to local affairs rather than a planned expansion.

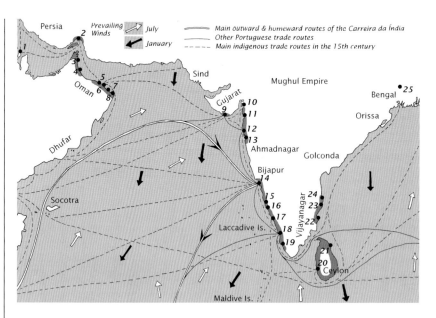

The *Estado da Índia*, western part: territory dominated by the Portuguese around the Arabian Sea and India, and outposts, at various times during the 16th and 17th ceturies.
(1) Bahrain; (2) Hormuz; (3) Khur Fakkan; (4) Suhar; (5) Matrah; (6) Muscat; (7) Qurayat; (8) Qalhat; (9) Diu; (10) Surat; (11) Daman; (12) Bassein; (13) Chaul; (14) Goa; (15) Mangalore; (16) Cannanore; (17) Calicut; (18) Cochin; (19) Quilon; (20) Colombo; (21) Trincomalee; (22) Nagapatam; (23) São Tomé; (24) Pulicate; (25) Hugli-Chinsura.

However, the Portuguese governors in Luanda faced a serious situation when large numbers of hungry African warriors emerged from the hills in roaming bands known as *jagas*. Then, in 1622, full-scale warfare broke out between the Portuguese coastal authorities and the extensive kingdom of Kongo. By this time the Portuguese were employing *jagas* as mercenaries, and although the better-equipped Portuguese forces won the war, their success undermined a trading relationship that had been built up over many decades. When Portuguese Africa was attacked by the Dutch the latter offered both firearms and training in their use to some African forces, resulting in higher Portuguese casualties (though not altering the final outcome).

The situation was different on the east coast of Africa, in what would become Mozambique. The initial phase of Portuguese aggression concluded with an assault upon Mombasa in 1524. Thereafter relations between the Portuguese coastal enclaves and the peoples of south-east Africa remained generally peaceful through most of the 16th century, despite occasional clashes.

In Ethiopia the situation was unique. Here Portuguese ambitions were for a while matched by some in the Ethiopian court; in 1520 the Portuguese ambassador Rodrigo da Lima found that the youthful Ethiopian Emperor Anbasa Segad Dawit II's own plans suited the Portuguese intention of closing the Bab al-Mandib strait to 'ruin Muslim prosperity'. When the Portuguese embassy returned to India both sides seemed satisfied; but in fact their grand strategy came to nothing, and it was the Muslim Sultan of Adal, Ahmad Ibn Ibrahim al-Ghazi (known as Gragn, 'the left-handed') who seized the initiative, invading Ethiopia and inflicting a devastating series of defeats upon Dawit II. With a vital ally apparently crumbling in East Africa, the Portuguese sent a small expeditionary force that eventually helped the Ethiopians to defeat Ahmad Gragn. Nevertheless, the Red Sea became a Muslim lake following the Ottoman Empire's seizure of Aden in 1538.

A Portuguese presence in South-East Asia was confirmed by their conquest of Malacca in 1511. Ten years later the small but prosperous Muslim sultanate of Sumatra in the northern part of that island also fell to the Portuguese, though they held it for only three years. Muslim power was in no sense broken, and the sultanate of Aceh soon rose to contest Portuguese dominance, until its own decline in the second half of the 17th century.

Far away in South America, the Portuguese adopted a different approach to that of their Spanish rivals, and in Brazil their interests remained almost entirely coastal. Not until the second half of the 16th century did many members of the Portuguese elite settle in Brazil, but then a sudden expansion of lucrative sugar production made the country far more attractive.

During the 17th century Portuguese strategy seemed to be failing. In 1616, for example, the English merchant Sir Thomas Roe wrote to the English East India Company stating that belligerent warfare and profitable trade were incompatible. Such 'armed trading' was, he maintained, causing the impoverishment of the Portuguese despite their apparently rich outposts in Asia. Nevertheless, the Portuguese *Estado da Índia* proved remarkably resilient during the bitter war with the Dutch, which was fought in almost every corner of the known world and lasted for more than half a century. This epic struggle eventually ended in 1663, after the Portuguese had confounded expectations by regaining much lost territory. That year the Portuguese Viceroy of Goa summed up the situation by recognizing that wars were not won with weapons alone: 'It is a well-known fact that the fortunes of war cannot be improved without men and money, and this is why we see so many disorders, so many tears and so many losses, because the King has only an empty Treasury and his vassals have no capital to help him'.

Tactics

Although the Portuguese military reforms of the later 14th century did not emphasize light cavalry *a la jinete* to the same degree as was seen in neighbouring Castile, light cavalry tactics featured prominently in 15th and 16th-century Portuguese warfare. Prior to that the traditional Portuguese emphasis had been on close co-operation between cavalry and infantry, as well as on the Islamic-Andalusian style of *zariba* field fortifications, as demonstrated at the battle of Aljubarrota in August 1385.

A much smaller affair during the Anglo-Portuguese invasion of north-western Castile illustrated defensive tactics in greater detail. According to a chronicle written a generation later, a small Portuguese force under Martim Vasques da Cunha was caught in open countryside by a larger Castilian force:

> Seeing themselves in the midst of a disaster, the Portuguese force began to shout, 'St George, St George! Portugal, Portugal!' Then they rushed to a small, low mound nearby... In fact, in that area there is no other high ground where they could have found any protection whatever. They all swiftly dismounted, positioning the animals around them, each tied to the next, and themselves in the centre, lance in hand, and back to back.' [While one man galloped away to summon help,] 'the

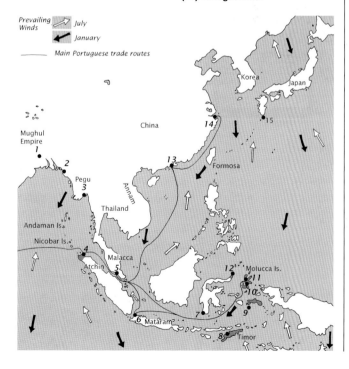

The *Estado da Índia,* eastern part: territory east of India dominated by the Portuguese, and outposts, at various times during the 16th and 17th centuries.
(1) Hugli-Chinsura;
(2) Chittagong; (3) Syriam;
(4) Pasei; (5) Malacca; (6) Banten;
(7) Macassar; (8) Lifao;
(9) Ambon; (10) Tidore;
(11) Ternate; (12) Manado;
(13) Macau; (14) Ningbo;
(15) Tanegashima.

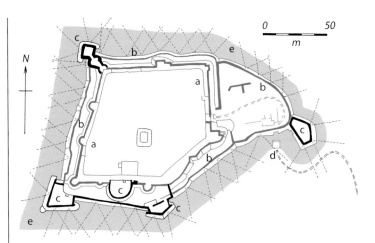

The Hormuzi and Portuguese fortress of Qal'at al-Bahrain was built on the site of ancient Tylos, which had become a major medieval Islamic town. The first significant defences were late medieval, but these were strengthened to face a Portuguese threat early in the 16th century. After conquering Bahrain the Portuguese added modern artillery bastions that greatly improved the fields of fire, here shown by broken lines. (a) Late medieval Islamic inner fortress; (b) Islamic outer fortress, 1518–19; (c) Portuguese bastions; (d) entrance; (e) dry moat. (After N. Faucherre *et al*)

Castilians surrounded the 17 men who remained, climbing the slope of that mound and hurling many lances at them – those that they carried with them as well as those they took from the foot-soldiers, of which a great number lay close by... Other attackers did not dare come too close because the Portuguese collected some of the lances thrown at them and threw them back.

Eventually a Portuguese relief force was seen approaching, and the Castilians retreated.

By the beginning of the 16th century the Portuguese had developed a highly effective form of what would today be called combined-operations warfare. This entailed making coastal landings with naval gunfire support – often in the face of immediate resistance – and these increasingly relied upon the latest forms of artillery and on infantry armed with matchlock arquebuses. For example, in 15th-century Morocco, the capture of Arzilah and Tangier by Portuguese seaborne assaults in 1471 relied heavily upon naval cannon-fire. However, this reliance upon the support of naval artillery meant that penetration further inland was often impossible.

By the time the Portuguese reached India and Arabia their amphibious assault tactics were probably the best in the world. The 16th century continued to see Portuguese combined operations along the Moroccan coast, of which a minor but well-documented example was a project to build a fort at al-M'amura to plug a gap between existing Portuguese outposts. This would supposedly pay for itself, by dominating a surrounding cereal-growing region; so an expedition of around 10,000 soldiers and colonists, commanded by Dom António de Noronha, sailed to Morocco in 1515. Having landed, the men promptly set about erecting a timber fortress (almost certainly partially prefabricated) and digging a protective ditch. Yet within a month this new outpost found itself surrounded by a large Moroccan army, equipped with cannon that inflicted such damage on the fort and on Portuguese ships in a neighbouring creek that the invaders hurriedly boarded a barge and sailed away.

In Arabia, some Portuguese expeditions were thwarted by inadequate information. For example, when a determinated assault was made upon Aden in 1513, submerged rocks prevented the small boats reaching the beach; the Portuguese arquebusiers had to wade through the surf, and by the time they got ashore their gunpowder was wet. Then the fortifications of Aden proved to be so strong that Portuguese cannonballs simply bounced off, and when the scaling ladders brought from India proved to be too short the invasion was called off. In fact, this failure at Aden undermined the myth of Portuguese invincibility, and thereafter resistance stiffened around much of the Indian Ocean.

During the 17th century Portuguese forces were more likely to be supporting existing coastal enclaves than carving out new ones. Following an uprising at Mombasa in East Africa in 1631, an expedition under

General Mora was sent to regain control. This time his fleet included galleys as well as large sailing ships. One detailed account stated that

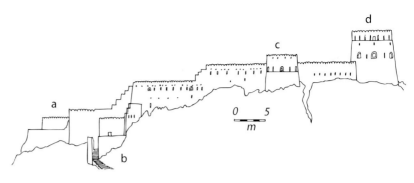

> On 8 January 1632 the fleet arrived... within sight of the fortress, which fired a shot but without harming anyone; and entering the mouth of the port, the General was warned that the [local] king had already placed a piece of artillery at a point where it had already done harm to a few ships... but as a galley and two ships had been placed to rake the position of this gun, the enemy, fearing a strong fleet, withdrew the gun, lest it should be lost.

Clearly the Portuguese still had superiority in numbers of artillery, if no longer a technological edge.

The Portuguese position in the East Indies was under even greater threat, and a notable setback was suffered when an *armada* under Viceroy Martin Afonso de Castro attacked Aceh in 1606. The viceroy had 3,012 men, of whom 2,392 were European or Eurasian soldiers and the rest sailors. He reportedly failed because he delayed disembarking his army off the bar at Aceh, thus giving the local forces time to organize a defence, and bitter resistance to the landing prevented the Portuguese from establishing more than a narrow beachhead. The situation looked so dangerous that de Castro was probably relieved when news reached him that the Dutch were besieging Malacca, thus giving him good reason to withdraw without losing face.

The Portuguese constructed watchtowers overlooking the harbour of Muttrah in Oman following their defeat at Hormuz in 1622, and these fortifications were subsequently strengthened by both the Portuguese and the Omanis. (a) North-western tower, probably Omani; (b) entrance through circuit wall, probably Omani; (c) Portuguese south-western tower; (d) Portuguese south-eastern tower. (After E. D'Errico)

WARSHIPS, EQUIPMENT & WEAPONS

It has been suggested that late medieval Portuguese 'royal galleons' formed the first truly national navy in Western Europe. However, the history of what became the Portuguese navy started considerably earlier, when the most effective fighting ships were galleys. These were primarily used for coastal raiding, and rarely attacked mercantile 'round ships' such as *nefs* (*nãos*) and cogs. Even so, in around 1381 France's Castilian allies were clearly more concerned about Portuguese galleys operating in the English Channel than they were about English warships. Other Portuguese ships were frequent visitors to English ports in the later 14th century, and these might find themselves 'arrested' to serve the English crown, transporting horses and men to and from the Continent. More detailed information about Portuguese ships confirms that the galleys that supported the Duke of Lancaster in his late 14th-century campaigns were notably large and strong, with 180 to 300 oarsmen, while the size and sturdiness of Portuguese *nãos* or transports similarly impressed their English allies. Following the adoption of cannon in naval warfare, war-galleys added an ability to mount heavier guns in their prows to their existing advantage of greater manoeuvrability. What could not

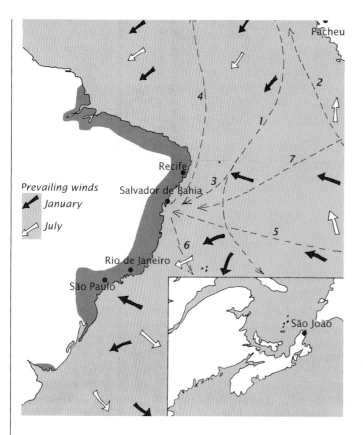

Pacheu

Recife

Salvador de Bahia

Rio de Janeiro

São Paulo

São João

Prevailing winds

January

July

The Portuguese Americas:
Portuguese territory and
outposts in Brazil, and South
Atlantic sea lanes, *c.*1650.
Main trade routes: (1) The
carreira da Índia, outwards
journey Portugal to India;
(2) return journey, India to
Portugal; (3) Portugal to Bahia,
Brazil; (4) Bahia to Portugal;
(5) Luanda, Angola, to Bahia;
(6) Bahia to Luanda; (7) Elmina,
West Africa, to Bahia.
Inset: The Portuguese settlement
of São João (Ingonish) on Cape
Breton Island, 1521–25.

be changed was the limited operational range of galleys; consequently, the Portuguese only started using them extensively in the Indian Ocean after achieving naval superiority and control of suitable ports.

The caravel may be the most famous type of ship used in the early days of Portuguese and Spanish maritime exploration, but it remained a small vessel, suitable for exploration but not for carrying the troops, supplies and horses required for overseas conquests. This duty fell to the deeper-draught carrack, which, by the 16th century, might have four decks and a crew of up to 200 men, equally divided between trained sailors and young apprentices known as *grumetes*. In 1633 Dom António de Ataíde suggested that the ideal crew for a carrack should consist of 18 officers (excluding the captain, who was classed as a soldier), 60 sailors, 60 *grumetes*, 4 pages or cabin-boys, and 26 gunners. Perhaps rather surprisingly, Portuguese ships were still widely considered undergunned even in the early 17th century. For example, in 1633 four-deck carracks being built for the passage to India had only 24 cannon of 10lb–11lb calibre. Six years later, however, a German traveller named Mandelslo noted that a Portuguese 'great ship', the largest form of carrack, had a complement of 600 'mariners and soldiers', and 64 brass guns.

Accommodation and conditions for such large numbers of men aboard ships making the six- to nine-month voyage to India were appalling, and the casualty rate could be horrific, especially amongst soldiers crammed between decks – in fact, the amount of space allocated for each man was so meagre that conditions were little better than those aboard later slave-trading ships.

Vessels often set sail with numerous live chickens, sheep and even a cow on board, but these would soon be eaten, as would any fresh fruit. Other food was often bad, with dried fish or salted meat having to be thrown overboard because it was rotten. Dried biscuit – the staple diet of long-distance mariners for centuries – might be over a year old even before sailing, and soon spoiled during a prolonged tropical voyage, while wine and water similarly deteriorated. On the other hand, nuts, dried fruit, other preserved vegetables and 'Flemish cheeses' lasted better, as did oil and 'sugared candies'. Such conditions lowered morale and led to suicidal despair among some new recruits, especially *degredados* and those with no experience of the sea. This in turn worsened the already bad sanitary conditions, as men abandoned hope of surviving the voyage.

By contrast, the prospect of action could raise the spirits, especially amongst the glory-seeking elite. The attitudes of the time were well described in an account of a clash between a Portuguese fleet commanded by Ruy Freyre d'Andrade and English ships off Hormuz on Christmas Day 1620. According to an English observer the Portuguese sailed out, and 'in a daring and braving manner invited us to an encounter, which we entertained with many Navall ceremonies, and putting out our collours of defiance, with the adorning our ships to answere their proportion of Gallantnesse, we made a brave show, as if we meant to entertaine death and slaughter with mirth and jollitie'. Eventually the ships *São Pedro* and *London* lay less than a musket-shot apart. Ruy Freyre took a glass of wine from a young servant and drank his opponent's health. His opposite number, named Shilling, replied in kind. Both men then hurled their goblets into the sea, and the fleets attacked each other to the accompaniment of drums and trumpets.

Arms and armour

Portugal was among the least industrialized countries in medieval Western Europe, and as a result most of its arms and armour were initially imported. Only the ex-Islamic south had much commerce and craftsmanship at the time of the Reconquista; however, by the 15th century a document called the *Organization of the Processions of Evora* referred to groups of skilled men including armourers, cutlers, spear- and shield-makers, saddlers, harness- and scabbard-makers, crossbowmen (who might have repaired, or even made their own weapons), and gunsmiths. It is notable that almost all the blacksmiths were Jewish. By the mid-15th century even recently colonized Madeira had its own arms industry, according to the Venetian traveller Luis de Cadamosto: 'The most excellent and beautiful bows and crossbow bolts of yew are made in this island, and are exported by ship to the mainland'.

A 16th-century Portuguese breastplate of the type used throughout the overseas territories. (Museu Nacional, Rio de Janeiro; photo R. Chartrand)

Until quite late in the 15th century Portuguese arms and armour remained somewhat distinctive, as well as old-fashioned, to the eyes of northern Europeans. From then on, however, they came under increasingly strong Italian influence because so much was imported from that country. Meanwhile the military equipment expected of members of the Portuguese Military Orders was steadily updated, so that by the 17th century every 'commander' was to have 'a horse and be properly armed for warfare, with a lance, buckler [small shield], armour and whatever else he could afford'. Ordinary brother-knights were to have 'armour, a helmet, an arquebus and a lance'. Inspections were held (though only every 13 years) to ensure that these men were equipped

This sword is said to be from the grave in Santarém of Pedro Álvares Cabral, the discoverer of Brazil. It was probably made between 1480 and 1500. (Rainer Daehnhardt Collection, Lisbon)

One of the more unusual infantry pole-arms used during the Late Medieval and Early Modern periods was the *croque;* this Portuguese example dates from the 16th century. Some of the distinctively European weapons used by the the Portuguese in their overseas conquests gave them an unexpected advantage, including the long infantry pike that had been developed in 15th-century Europe for defence against cavalry. On one occasion in Malacca in 1511, when the Portuguese faced some terrifying war-elephants, squads of disciplined pikemen thrust at the animals' eyes, and, when the elephants reared in panic, at their 'tender parts'. (Rainer Daehnhardt Collection, Lisbon)

according to their station, and substantial fines were imposed for failure.

The equipment of ordinary soldiers varied according to the place in which they served, but they were almost invariably much better armed and protected than indigenous warriors. As in so many later colonial wars, the results could be dramatic even when the Europeans and their local allies were hugely outnumbered. One such outcome was seen in 1580, when a few Portuguese soldiers defeated the King of Angola. When asked how such a success was possible, Duarte Lopés wrote:

I reply that it might easily happen, seeing that … the blacks wore no clothing, had no defensive weapons and only bows and daggers as offensive ones. Whereas our small numbers of men were well covered with quilted jerkins lined with cotton, and firmly double-sewn, which protected their arms and reached down to the knees. Their heads are covered with caps of this same material, which are proof against arrows and daggers… One cavalry soldier is equal to a hundred blacks, who are greatly afraid of horsemen and, above all, of those who fire the arquebuses and artillery pieces, which cause them extreme terror.

The Islamic *Tarīkh Shanbal* described the psychological impact of Portuguese weaponry when the latter attacked Calicut in 1509/10: 'Then as the Franks approached the aforementioned city, [the local people] were stricken with panic … because of the equipment, weapons, and great number of men they perceived… So they fled … and the Franks entered the town'. Not that the Portuguese soldiers always had the equipment they were supposed to carry. Some resorted to stealing weaponry that had been issued solely for use during the voyage, as the sailing orders for a mid-17th century *armada* warned:

All the weapons on board must be inspected, cleaned and repaired by the armourers every 15 days… Soldiers who have been issued with weapons on the voyage are apt to try to retain them at the end, refusing to hand them back to the master-at-arms. This abuse cannot be tolerated, and effective measures must be taken to ensure that all these weapons are collected before the soldiers disembark at Goa.

Portugal and its Muslim Andalusian foes had long used large and complex crossbows, which also became the most important weapons aboard Portuguese ships from the later 13th century onwards. Initially these were probably of a relatively heavy, long-range type with a simple bow made of yew and spanned using both feet. This was known as an *'aqqara* in Andalus and North Africa, where its one-piece bowstave made it particularly suitable for service at sea – staves of composite construction suffered in damp conditions. Crossbows with steel staves became increasingly common during the 15th century, but they remained expensive to manufacture in large numbers.

Firearms

The Iberian peninsula and North Africa saw significant experimentation in the use of gunpowder and firearms during the 14th and 15th centuries. *Tiros do fogo* hand-held guns were used during King Duarte's unsuccessful expedition against Tangier in 1437, and his successor Afonso V is widely credited with modernizing Portugal's arsenal of firearms. He recruited skilled craftsmen from Flanders and Germany, who cast up-to-date bronze cannon with better range and accuracy than the old wrought-iron guns. Light cannon and hand-held weapons feature prominently in the Pastrana Tapestries, which celebrate a Portuguese invasion of Morocco in 1470. Thereafter the importance of hand-held guns increased significantly, since the technological superiority of Portugal's small and isolated colonial garrisons was often the only advantage they had.

The Portuguese had a significant influence upon Ethiopian military architecture, though most of that country's 17th-century fortifications were made after the Portuguese left. They include fortified monasteries, such as this one at Debre Birhan Selassie in Gondar. (Photo Ansha Nega)

Nevertheless, the Portuguese faced enemies who were similarly eager to obtain modern weapons, especially in Morocco. The chonicler Garcia de Resende, writing in the first half of the 16th century, regretted the impact of firearms during the Moroccan campaigns: 'There have been more inventions of artillery in our days than in all time past. We do not cease from having today great men, as in past years; however, if they show themselves to be better than average, they are killed within the hour, before achieving fame. The mighty artillery of today has destroyed chivalry'.

The limitations of Portugal's somewhat light guns, especially those used at sea, were eventually remedied by the gun-foundry of Manuel Tavares Bocarro, who was Governor of Macau in China from 1654 to 1664. It operated from around 1627 to 1664, and produced an astonishing number of high-quality iron and bronze weapons. Three generations of the Bocarro family manufactured guns, which were in demand by friend and foe alike around the coasts of Asia. Elsewhere some Portuguese garrison commanders continued to complain about inadequate artillery. In Tangier the garrison's desperate attempts to melt down and recast their existing guns were not very successful. Meanwhile, the capability to make cannon spread amongst non-European peoples, often taught by the Portuguese and Dutch. Though these were usually of bronze rather than iron, the results were good enough for the Portuguese to happily re-use captured locally-made guns during the 17th century.

SELECT BIBLIOGRAPHY

Azurara, Gomes Eannes de, (tr. B. Miall), *Conquests and Discoveries of Henry the Navigator: being the chronicles of Azurara* (London, 1936)

Battell, A. (ed. E.G. Ravenstein), *The Strange Adventures of Andrew Battell of Leigh in Angola and the Adjoining Regions* (London, 1901)

Bessa, C., 'Le Portugal 1383–1385: crise, art militaire et consolidation de l'indépendence', in P. Konieczny (ed), *From Crécy to Mohács, Warfare in the Late Middle Ages* (Vienna, 1997) pp.28–50

Bethencourt, F., *Portuguese Oceanic Expansion* (Cambridge, 2007)

Botelho de Costa Veiga, A., 'De Estramoz a Aljubarrota. Quinze dias de operaçãoes de Nun'Alvarez', in *O Instituto*, 80 (1930) & 81 (1931)

Bovill, E.W., *The Battle of Alcazar: An account of the defeat of Don Sebastian of Portugal at el-Kasr el-Kebir* (London, 1952)

Boxer, C.R., 'The Achinese attack on Malacca in 1629, as described in contemporary Portuguese sources', in J. Bastin & R. Roolvink (eds.), *Malayan and Indonesian Studies* (Oxford, 1964) pp.105–121

Boxer, C.R., 'Asian Potentates and European Artillery in the 16th–18th Centuries', in *Journal of the Malay Branch of the Royal Asiatic Society*, 38 (1966) p.157

Boxer, C.R., *The Portuguese Seaborne Empire, 1415–1825* (London, 1969)

Boxer, C.R., 'Dom Jorge de Meneses Baroche and the Battle of Mulleriyáwa, 1560', in *Mare Luso-Indicum*, 3 (1976) pp.85–97

Boxer, C.R., 'The Sailing Orders for the Portuguese East-Indiamen of 1640 and 1646', in *Terrae Incognitae*, 12 (1980)

Coates, T.J., *Convicts and Orphans. Forced and State-Sponsored Colonizers in the Portuguese Empire, 1550–1755* (Stanford, 2001)

Da Fonseca, L.A., 'The Portuguese Military Orders and the Oceanic Navigations: From Piracy to Empire', in J. Upton-Ward (ed.), *The Military Orders, Volume 4. On Land and by Sea* (Aldershot, 2008) pp.63–73

Dames, M.L., 'The Portuguese and the Turks in the Indian Ocean in the 16th Century', in *Journal of the Royal Asiatic Society* (1921) pp.1–28

De Silva, C.R., *The Portuguese in Ceylon, 1617–1638* (Colombo, 1972)

Diffie, B.W., & G.D. Winius, *Foundations of the Portuguese Empire, 1415–1580* (Minneapolis, 1977)

Disney, A.R., *The Portuguese in India and Other States, 1500–1700* (Aldershot, 2009)

Disney, A.R., 'Vasco da Gama's Reputation for Violence: The Alleged Atrocities at Calicut in 1502', in *Indica*, 32 (1995) pp.11–28

Disney, A.R., *Twilight of the Pepper Empire* (London, 1978)

Domingues, F.C., 'The State of Portuguese Naval Forces in the Sixteenth Century', in J.B. Hattendorf & R.W. Unger (eds.), *War at Sea in the Middle Ages and the Renaissance* (Woodbridge, 2003) pp.187–197

Do Paço, A., 'The Battle of Aljubarrota', in *Antiquity*, 37 (1963) pp.264–269

Donovan, B.M., 'The Discovery and Conquest of the Brazilian Frontier', in G.D. Winius (ed.), *Portugal, The Pathfinder: Journeys from the Medieval towards the Modern World 1300–ca.1600* (Madison, 1995) pp.229–246

Duarte, Dom (tr. A.F. Preto), *The Royal Book of Jousting, Horsemanship and Knightly Combat* (Highland Village, 2005)

Dutra, F.A., *Military Orders in the Early Modern Portuguese World* (Aldershot, 2006)

Faucherre, N., 'The Hormuzi-Portuguese Fortress, new fortress of Qal'at al-Bahrain', in M. Kervran et al (eds.), *Qal'at al-Bahrain: A Trading and Military Outpost* (Turnhout, 2005) pp.345–426

Freeman-Grenville, G.S.P., *The East African Coast. Select Documents from the first to the earlier nineteenth century* (Oxford, 1962)

Freeman-Grenville, G.S.P., *The Mombasa Rising against the Portuguese, 1631* (Oxford, 1980)

Greenlee, W.B., *The Voyage of Pedro Alvares Cabral to Brazil and India, from Contemporary documents and narratives* (New Delhi, 1995)

Hutchinson, A., 'Nun' Álvares Pereira, A Portuguese Hero in the Arthurian Mould', in T.F. Earle & N. Griffin (eds.), *Portuguese, Brazilian, and African Studies* (Warminster, 1995) pp.55–68

Lawrence, A.W., *Trade Castles and Forts of West Africa* (London, 1963)

Lopes, F., *The English in Portugal 1367–87* (Warminster, 1988)

Matos, G. de M., *Memoria sobreo alcance das armas usadas nos seculos XV a XVII* (Lisbon, 1944)

Monteiro, J.G., 'The Battle of Aljubarrota (1385): A Reassessment', in *Journal of Medieval Military History*, 7 (2009) pp.75–103

Moser, G.M., 'The Grumbling Veterans of an Empire', in A. Hower & R.A. Preto-Rodas (eds.), *Empire in Transition; the Portuguese World in the Time of Camões* (Gainsville, 1985)

Munro, D.C., 'A Venetian Memorandum of the Power and Revenues of the States of Europe in the 1420s', in *Translations and Reprints from the Original Sources of European History, vol. 3* (Philadelphia, 1907) pp.13–18.

Newitt, M., *The Portuguese in West Africa, 1415–1670* (Cambridge, 2010)

Pearson, M.N., *Port Cities and Intruders. The Swahili Coast, India, and Portugal in the Early Modern Period* (Baltimore, 1998)

Peele, G., 'The Battell of Alcazer, Fought in Barbarie…', in (ed. anon.) *The Battle of Alcazar 1597; Malone Society Reprints* (London, 1907)

Prestage, E. (ed.), *Chapters in Anglo-Portuguese Relations* (Watford, 1935)

Prestage, E. (tr.), *The Chronicles of Fernao Lopés and Gomes Eannes de Zurara* (Watford, 1928)

Preto-Rodas, R.A. (ed.), *Empire in Transition: The Portuguese World in the Time of Camões* (Gainesville, 1985)

Ricard, R., *Etudes sur l'histoire des Portugais au Maroc* (Coimbra, 1955)

Russell, P.E., 'Portuguese galleys in the service of Richard II, 1385–1389', in P.E. Russell, *Portugal, Spain and the African Atlantic, 1343–1490* (Aldershot, 1995)

Serjeant, R.B., *The Portuguese off the South Arabian Coast: Hadrami chronicles* (Oxford, 1963)

Trim, D., 'Early Modern Colonial Warfare and the Campaign of Alcazarquivir, 1578', in *Small Wars and Insurgencies*, 8 (1997) pp.1–34

Vogt, J. 'Saint Barbara's Legions: Portuguese Artillery in the Struggle for Morocco, 1415–1578', in *Military Affairs*, 41 (1977) pp.178–182

Welch, S.R., *Portuguese rule and Spanish crown in South Africa, 1581–1640* (Cape Town, 1950)

PLATE COMMENTARIES

A: PORTUGAL, c.1340's–1380's

Chronologically, these figures run from right to left:

A1: Portuguese sergeant, mid-14th century

With his old-fashioned helmet, mail hauberk and large 'mantlet' form of shield, this figure represents the archaic military equipment that persisted in Portugal well into the 14th century, though some aspects of his clothing are more up-to-date than his armour. However, the Catalan manuscript upon which this figure is largely based may have exaggerated what many other Europeans regarded as the 'backward' character of Portugal.

A2: Portuguese knight, mid-14th century

Even in Portugal itself, artists often portrayed warriors wearing armour in ways that would have struck their neighbours as unusual, as well as reflecting a continuing strong military influence from the country's Andalusian-Islamic past. For example, this man wears a mail coif over his cervelliére helmet – an outdated habit elsewhere in Europe. However, reliance on mail protection with minimal plate armour, and use of an old-fashioned great helm, was seen in other parts of the Iberian peninsula, as was the horse's caparison without protective elements.

A3: Portuguese knight, later 14th century

Portugal's adoption of French and English military styles in the later 14th century did not replace distinctive local fashions. Some of the latter continued to reflect Islamic Granada and even North Africa; for example, the scale-lined 'epaulettes' and thigh-protecting tassets of the brigandine were distinctively Portuguese. They represented an extensive but relatively light form of armour that would endure for centuries, and would to some extent answer the climatic demands of Portugal's tropical empire.

B: CANARY ISLANDS, EARLY 15th CENTURY

B1: Portuguese knight

Castile rather than Portugal eventually dominated the Canary Islands, but Portuguese explorers were among the first to encounter the essentially Neolithic culture of the indigenous Guanche peoples. This came as a huge surprise to European explorers, who had expected to face European- or Islamic-style armies and even fortified cities. With his scale-lined brigandine, an open-faced salet helmet, full leg harness and plate arm defences without gauntlets, this Portuguese knight reflects a vastly more advanced military culture than that of the Guanches. Note too the falchion-style sword,

B2: Portuguese hand-gunner

An infantryman armed with a hand-gun would have been an even more astonishing sight to the local inhabitants. Beneath his hat he wears a simple salet with a slightly corrugated skull, and he has a thickly quilted jacket. The persistence of Andalusian-Islamic traditions, including a light sword and a hardened leather *adarga* shield, proved suitable for Portuguese soldiers as they pressed ever further southwards.

B3: Portuguese scribe, c.1400

The increasing cultural, commercial and technological contacts between Portugal and Italian maritime powers such as Genoa meant that the Portuguese had access to the latest cartographical knowledge. The educated elite also rapidly came to terms with the strange peoples, oceans, lands and climates that they discovered.

B4: Gaunche native

Nevertheless, sights like a local Guanche vaulting across precipitous gulleys by using a 'leaping pole' must have astonished even the most open-minded.

C: EXPLORATION & SLAVE-RAIDING, MID 15th CENTURY

C1: Portuguese commander

The profits which flowed into Portugal after the first explorers

A three-masted ship with the arms of Portugal on its mainsail, on a superb lustre-ware ceramic probably made in Manises, eastern Spain, in c.1400 (Victoria & Albert Museum, London)

Afonfo·von·gots·
gnaden·kūng·:·
·zū·portgal·vnd·
·algarbe·:·her·zū·
·fept·vnd··zū·al·
·gogvro·

King Afonso V, who ruled Portugal from 1458 to 1471. This is a very clear image of the silhouette of a fashionable aristocratic costume of the later 15th century. (*Georg of Ehingen Manuscript*, Württembergische Landesbibliothek, Ms. Hist. 4, f. 141, Stuttgart)

pushed beyond the Canary Islands made it one of the richest countries in Western Europe. This was soon reflected in Portuguese armies and fleets, from more abundant and up-to-date military equipment to larger and more numerous ships. The senior officer shown here wears typical European arms and armour, though in a limited amount because he is serving aboard ship.

C2: Portuguese crossbowman
The distinctive variations upon basic 15th-century European light armour that became a feature of Portuguese military equipment are very noticeable on this figure. His tall iron helmet was probably of North African Islamic origin, and his scale-lined brigandine was imported from Germany, but the iron bars laced to his forearms and lower legs below the plate elbow and knee defences, as a defence against cutting blows, seem to be distinctly Portuguese.

C3: Portuguese sailor
Tall hats with their crowns bent forward were fashionable in mid-15th century Portugal, though this example is unusual in having a separate cover laced to the basic hat. The man's mail shirt is a form more commonly worn by men-at-arms beneath other armour. Perhaps it is a battlefield trophy, along with an elaborate belt normally associated with a member of the knightly elite, while the sword still shows residual Andalusian

influence.

The large wooden astrolabe (navigation table) that the crossbowman and sailor have dismounted from its stand is taken from a drawing of a Portuguese ship. Among the gear stacked at bottom right, the sailor's *adarga* shield is a large version of the North African *daraqa*; the crossbow may be either of Portuguese manufacture or imported from Spain; and the handgun, with its serpentine trigger mechanism, is of the latest European design.

D: INVASION OF MOROCCO, LATE 15th CENTURY

D1: Portuguese man-at-arms
Portuguese attempts to seize control of Morocco were portrayed in various works of art, notably the tapestries now preserved at Pastrana, Spain. The huge sums of money spent on these doomed crusades, and the importance given to the splendid appearance of the armies involved, is confirmed in the written sources. This man-at-arms is a brother knight of the Portuguese Military Order of Aviz. His steel helmet is entirely covered with gold-embroidered velvet, and his breastplate is etched with the sign of the Christian cross. Only his broad-bladed, relatively short-hafted spear seems to be a concession to the style of fast-moving cavalry warfare characteristic of these North African campaigns.

D2: Portuguese infantryman
By the late 15th century some infantry elements in Portuguese armies formed a professional elite, being as well equipped as the cavalry. Certain distinctive local fashions persisted and would be steadily updated. The substantial upper-arm defences laced to the shoulders of this soldier's brigandine are an example. The hilt of his sword is in a style that became popular throughout the Iberian peninsula and may have been of Moorish origin, while his large leather shield is a development of the earlier *adarga*, though with metallic reinforcements.

D3: Portuguese standard-bearer
Standard-bearers were always well equipped, often with decorative arms and elaborate horse-armour. Being a focus of attention for friend and foe alike, they had to be both highly visible and well armoured. This horseman, carrying the banner of the Military Order of Aviz, has the best available imported Italian armour, though his use of a light brigandine was probably a concession to the Moroccan climate. In contrast, plated horse-armour covered in rich brocade, plus a neck-covering pol, head-protecting chamfron and a saddle partly covered with steel plates, meant that his mount was constantly in danger of heat exhaustion. It is worth noting that his sword too has rings beneath the quillons to protect the forefinger while fencing in what was called an 'Italian style'; in reality this fashion reached Europe from the Islamic world, and may have originated in India.

E: ETHIOPIA, EARLY 16th CENTURY

E1: Portuguese man-at-arms
Some of the survivors of a battle with the Muslim Ethiopian forces of Ahmad Gragn remained to help the Christian Ethiopians eventually defeat their local foes. This man-at-arms has the simple munitions armour issued to forces across the expanding Portuguese maritime empire. Beneath a broad-brimmed steel helmet and substantial bevor to protect his

A Portuguese *fidalgo* or military officer, clearly shown off-duty in this early 17th-century Mughul Indian painting. Compare this image with Plate G3. (Victoria & Albert Museum, inv. IM.9–1913, London)

throat, he wears a mail gorget with a padded lining. Beneath his plate cuirass with additional plackart belly protection he has a mail haubergeon. Lacking leg armour, he wears fashionably 'slashed' kid leather hose, and a pronounced cod-piece beneath the haubergeon.

E2: Portuguese infantryman
Perhaps having lost his helmet, this footsoldier wears what appears to be a padded arming cap. German-made brigandines were widely exported, and this unusual form that included full-length sleeves is known to have been used in the Iberian peninsula. His abundantly slashed leather 'upper stocks' or hose are laced up in four separate places. In addition to a good quality sword with a complex hilt, he might carry a large-bladed, very long-hafted pole-axe.

E3: Aristocratic Ethiopian cavalryman
The strongest military influences upon the powerful but isolated Christian kingdom of Abyssinia came from neighbouring Islamic regions. The helmet worn by this cavalryman has been claimed as medieval Egyptian, though it was probably made in the Sudan or Ethiopia itself. Short-sleeved mail shirts were used throughout the Middle East and along the southern fringes of the Sahara desert, while quilted armour for man and horse had been used throughout all these regions for centuries. The riding boots are based on a late medieval example found in Christian Nubia, which, though made of padded cloth, are shaped like the leather riding boots used throughout the Islamic world.

F: BRAZIL, 16th CENTURY
F1: Brazilian Tupinamba chief
Early Portuguese illustrations of the indigenous peoples of South America generally showed both sexes virtually naked, though with an elite wearing clothing decorated with the feathers of tropical birds. A few items such as this chieftain's feathered headdress survive in museums. The weaponry of such tribesmen may have been primitive by European standards, but it certainly included powerful bows. A few illustrations showing more sophisticated costume were once thought to reflect Portuguese influence or even the artist's own imagination. However, recent archaeological research shows that several Brazilian cultures were far more sophisticated than previously thought, and that early Portuguese illustrations of indigenous elites were by no means fanciful.

F2: Brazilian-Portuguese nobleman, mid-16th century
A sugar industry brought sudden prosperity to the expanding Portuguese settlements in Brazil, as reflected in this Luso-Brazilian *senhor*'s armour, costume and horse-harness. His cuirass is of a laminated form. Laminations also give greater flexibility to the tassets and cuisses that protect his hips and thighs, and, of course, to his gauntlets. His helmet, carried by his retainer, is an early form of visored burgonet. His coat bears the cross of the Portuguese branch of the Order of Santiago, later known as the Order of St James of the Sword.

F3: Afro-Brazilian retainer, late 16th century
Men of non-European origin, and more especially of mixed African-Portuguese parentage, soon played a prominent military role in Brazil; some reached high command, and became national heroes during the long 17th-century struggle against Dutch invasion. Whatever their rank, their costume and equipment was identical to that of their European compatriots. This musketeer wears a morion helmet, a substantial mail tippet and a quilted jack. In addition to a heavy matchlock arquebus he is armed with a heavy sword, and would also carry a substantial dagger at his right side.

G: INDIAN OCEAN, LATE 16th–EARLY 17th CENTURY
G1: Goan-Indian soldier in Portuguese service
Local soldiers played a significant role in the defence of Portuguese enclaves on the Indian coast, those in Goa often being recruited from the indigenous Christian population. Goa also became a significant arms-manufacturing centre, producing not only cannon but also armour, such as this

A carved ivory salt-cellar in Bibi-Portuguese style from Nigeria, early 16th century. It shows European soldiers perhaps wearing quilted armour including (foreground) thigh defences, compare with Plate H1. (Metropolitan Museum of Art, inv. 1972.63, New York)

man's magnificently decorated helmet. His weapons are, however, entirely south Indian, and include a massive single-stave bow which Portuguese observers described as being 'like those of the English'.

G2: Portuguese man-at-arms
The wealth of Portugal's *Estado da Índia* is shown in this reconstruction. The man-at-arms – inspecting the edge achieved by use of the barrow-mounted sharpening-stone in the background – is equipped as a heavy cavalryman or cuirassier. His armour represents the final flowering of a long-

established Western European tradition that was already unable to protect the wearer from gunfire. The only concession to such changes are his open-faced burgonet helmet (laid aside, right) and the limited lower-leg defences, which permit greater control of his horse. By this date a pair of deep pistol holsters would be attached to the front of his saddle; these weapons had been accepted as necessary even in combats between opposing cavalry.

G3: Portuguese soldier, late 16th century
Mughul Indian illustrations of Portuguese soldiers often show them 'off duty', in items of costume that rarely appear in more formal European illustrations. They include this man's open-necked shirt with a broad lace collar, unbuttoned jacket with removable sleeves, and baggy trousers. His morion helmet is of one-piece construction; his sword is a fine weapon with an all-steel hilt, and his wheel-lock musket could be used either on foot or on horseback. Resting on a massive multi-barrel *ribaudequin*-style artillery piece, he whiles away his afternoon playing a Portuguese bagpipe.

H: SOUTHERN AFRICA, c.1600–1650
H1: Portuguese soldier
During the 17th century some of the Portuguese outposts in southern Africa saw considerable fighting against foes who greatly outnumbered the garrisons. Written sources indicate that quilted armour was widely used by Portuguese troops in this theatre. Quilted jacks like this one were commonplace across early 17th-century Europe, but the identity of the quilted helmets is less clear – the quilted head protections widely used in India may have been adopted by some Portuguese because they were more suited to the tropical climate. This man's quilted leg defences are based on an ivory carving that was probably made in Goa, as was his carved powder horn. By contrast, the ivory powder flasks hanging from the bandolier of his stacked equipment (background) were made somewhere in Portuguese-ruled Africa.

H2: African warrior in Portuguese service
An illustrated Portuguese manuscript made by a local artist somewhere in India illustrates most of the known peoples around the Indian Ocean. Several African peoples are included, and, although their costume and weaponry were less varied than those illustrated for Asian peoples, the artist was at pains to highlight local characteristics. Hence this figure is given the simple costume and relatively short bow of a warrior from one of the powerful interior kingdoms of southern Africa. The bow was probably of composite construction, and may have been made in one of the Islamic coastal cities of what is now Mozambique, whereas the broad-bladed *asagai* was used throughout most of sub-Saharan Africa.

H3: Portuguese officer, c.1650
India was the posting with the greatest potential for making money, while Portuguese outposts in southern Africa tended to be both less profitable and even unhealthier. In contrast to the Portuguese officer in Plate G2, this man is protected by a gorget (which already served as a mark of rank as much as a protection) plus steel breast- and back-plates, over a thick, short-sleeved coat of buff leather. His status is shown by his baton of command and by the elaborate gilded hilt of his rapier.

INDEX

References to illustrations are shown in **bold**.
Plates are shown with page and caption
locators in brackets.